HOMELAND SECURITY
OPERATIONAL ANALYSIS CENTER

Developing Recovery Options for Puerto Rico's Economic and Disaster Recovery Plan

Process and Methodology

HSOAC PUERTO RICO RECOVERY TEAM

Published in 2020

HSOAC Puerto Rico Recovery Team

Cross-Sector Teams

Project Leadership
Cynthia R. Cook, project lead
Anu Narayanan, deputy
Justin Hodiak, deputy
Shoshana R. Shelton

Quality Assurance
Carrie M. Farmer

Recovery Plan Development
Joie D. Acosta, lead
Amanda Wicker, deputy
Melissa L. Finucane

Innovation
Jon Schmid, lead
Christopher K. Gilmore
Karishma V. Patel
Li Ang Zhang

Cross-Sector Integration
Melissa L. Finucane, lead
Katie Whipkey, deputy

Forward Team
Christopher M. Schnaubelt, lead
Jaime L. Hastings, deputy

Damage and Needs Assessment
Jordan R. Fischbach, lead
Linnea Warren May, deputy
Lisa S. Meredith
Shoshana R. Shelton
Devin Tierney
Christine Anne Vaughan
Katie Whipkey

Cost Analysis and Funding Sources
Michael Kennedy, lead
David Metz, deputy
Elaine K. Dezenski
Cedric N. Kenney
Robert S. Leonard
Fred Timson

Communications
Chandra Garber, lead
Melissa Bauman
Kristin J. Leuschner
Libby May
Sydne Newberry
Lauren Skrabala
Dori Walker

Decision Support
David G. Groves, lead
Nidhi Kalra
James Syme

Courses of Action
Nicholas Burger, lead
David G. Groves
Justin Hodiak
Karishma V. Patel
Aaron Strong
Katie Whipkey

Sector Teams

Economics
Craig A. Bond, lead
Aaron Strong, deputy
Megan Andrew
John S. Crown*
Kathryn Edwards
Gabriella C. Gonzalez
Italo A. Gutierrez
Jill E. Luoto
Karishma V. Patel
Kyle Pratt
Alexander D. Rothenberg
Troy D. Smith
Patricia K. Tong
Melanie A. Zaber

Energy
Aimee E. Curtright, lead
Martha V. Merrill, deputy*
Timothy R. Gulden
Kelly Klima
Geoffrey McGovern
Evan D. Peet
Lindsey Polley
Sara Turner

Natural and Cultural Resources
Susan A. Resetar, lead
Abbie Tingstad, deputy
Katherine Anania
Beth E. Lachman
Miriam Elizabeth Marlier
James V. Marrone
Joshua Mendelsohn*

Housing
Noreen Clancy, lead
Lloyd Dixon, deputy
Dan Elinoff*
Kathryn Kuznitsky
Sean McKenna
Cordaye Ogletree

Health and Social Services
Christopher Nelson, lead
Anita Chandra, deputy
Mahshid Abir
Edward W. Chan
Jaime Madrigano
Terry Marsh*
Nupur Nanda
Jamie Ryan
Molly M. Simmons
Michelle D. Ziegler*

Education
Christopher Nelson, lead
Anita Chandra, deputy
Drew M. Anderson
Megan Andrew
Lynn A. Karoly
Terry Marsh*
Robert F. Murphy
Nupur Nanda
Andrea Prado Tuma
Troy D. Smith
Anamarie A. Whitaker
Michelle D. Ziegler*

Water
Benjamin Lee Preston, lead
Michelle E. Miro, deputy
Paul Brenner*
David Catt
Christopher K. Gilmore
Alexandra Huttinger
Jaime Madrigano
John F. Raffensperger

Municipalities
Blas Nuñez-Neto, lead
Andrew Lauland, deputy
Jair Aguirre
Gabriela Castro
Italo A. Gutierrez
Marielena Lara
Erika Meza
Chelsey Miranda*
Etienne Rosas

Communications and Information Technology
Amado Cordova, lead*
Ryan Consaul, deputy
John Bordeaux
Ajay Kochhar
Ricardo Sanchez
Karlyn D. Stanley

Transportation
Liisa Ecola, lead
Kenneth Kuhn, deputy
Thomas F. Atkin
Mark Barrett
Eric Cooper
Aaron C. Davenport
Jeffrey Kendall*
Alexander D. Rothenberg

Public Buildings
Tom LaTourrette, lead
Benjamin M. Miller, deputy
Krista S. Langeland
Andrew Lauland
Nupur Nanda
Teddy Ulin*
Kristin Van Abel

* Forward team liaison.

iii

Preface

On September 19 and 20, 2017, Hurricane Maria caused widespread destruction across the U.S. Commonwealth of Puerto Rico. Making landfall just two weeks after Hurricane Irma, Maria—a strong Category 4 storm—significantly damaged local infrastructure and interrupted the provision of essential and nonessential services. On September 20, 2017, President Donald Trump signed a major disaster declaration for Hurricane Maria (Federal Emergency Management Agency [FEMA], 2017) under the Robert T. Stafford Disaster Relief and Emergency Assistance Act (Pub. L. 100-707, 1988). In the aftermath of Hurricanes Irma and Maria, FEMA has been working closely with the government of Puerto Rico and its municipalities; other federal agencies; private-sector entities; and voluntary, faith-based, and community organizations to stabilize Puerto Rico. Attention is now turning to the commonwealth's long-term recovery needs.

A supplemental appropriations bill, passed by Congress on February 8, 2018, required the governor of Puerto Rico, in coordination with FEMA, the U.S. Department of Treasury, the U.S. Department of Energy, and other federal agencies with responsibilities under the National Disaster Recovery Framework, to submit a report to Congress, within 180 days of enactment of the legislation, that describes Puerto Rico's 12- and 24-month economic and disaster recovery plan. The government of Puerto Rico's recovery plan (Governor of Puerto Rico, 2018a) lays out the priorities, goals, and expected outcomes of the recovery effort in Puerto Rico. The plan was developed in coordination with the Financial Oversight and Management Board for Puerto Rico (created under the Puerto Rico Oversight, Management, and Economic Stability Act of 2016), the federal interagency Recovery Support Function teams and field coordinators, and key partners from private and nongovernmental entities, using an agile process to identify recovery solutions.

FEMA turned to the Homeland Security Operational Analysis Center (HSOAC), a federally funded research and development center (FFRDC) run by the RAND Corporation under contract with the U.S. Department of Homeland Security (DHS), to work with the government of Puerto Rico, FEMA and other federal agencies, and other stakeholders in support of the writing of this plan. This report summarizes the strategic planning process that HSOAC used to support the government of Puerto Rico in its development of the recovery plan. The report describes HSOAC's approach to gathering information and conducting analysis to produce a detailed damage and needs assessment report (Fischbach et al., 2020) and to outline an array of potential recovery actions (termed *courses of action* [COAs] in this effort) that Puerto Rico could take to repair damage from the hurricanes and address longer-term economic recovery needs. HSOAC developed these COAs based on input from, and in partnership with, external stakeholders and experts, internal experts, and the government of Puerto Rico; the COAs were also informed by findings in the damage and needs assessment. Although the work described in this report enabled planning activities related to these COAs, data and time constraints limited the team's analysis of the benefits and costs. As a result, choosing among the COAs and implementing them will require additional analysis.

This report also describes a decision support tool that HSOAC designed to facilitate interaction between the HSOAC team; officials from the government of Puerto Rico; and other stakeholders, including FEMA and other federal departments. Officials from the government of Puerto Rico and federal partners used the tool to review and select portfolios of COAs that could meet their objectives and be the basis for the recovery plan.

This report describes work conducted between February and July 2018. This research was sponsored by FEMA and conducted within the Strategy, Policy, and Operations Program of the HSOAC FFRDC. More information about HSOAC's contribution to planning for recovery in Puerto Rico, along with links to other reports being published as part of this series, can be found at www.rand.org/hsoac/puerto-rico-recovery.

About the Homeland Security Operational Analysis Center

The Homeland Security Act of 2002 (Section 305 of Public Law 107-296, as codified at 6 U.S.C. § 185), authorizes the Secretary of Homeland Security, acting through the Under Secretary for Science and Technology, to establish one or more FFRDCs to provide independent analysis of homeland security issues. The RAND Corporation operates HSOAC as an FFRDC for the DHS under contract HSHQDC-16-D-00007.

The HSOAC FFRDC provides the government with independent and objective analysis and advice in core areas important to DHS in support of policy development, decisionmaking, and new ideas on issues of significance. The HSOAC FFRDC also works with and supports other federal, state, local, tribal, and public- and private-sector organizations that make up the homeland security enterprise. The HSOAC FFRDC's research is undertaken by mutual consent with DHS and is organized as a set of discrete tasks. This report presents the Project Management Plan HSOAC will use to undertake the Task Order 70FBR218F00000032, "Puerto Rico Economic & Disaster Recovery Plan: Integration and Analytic Support."

The results presented in this report do not necessarily reflect official DHS opinion or policy. For more information on HSOAC, see www.rand.org/hsoac. For more information on this publication, see www.rand.org/t/RR2597.

Contents

HSOAC Puerto Rico Recovery Team.. iii

Preface.. iv

Figures.. vii

Tables viii

Summary ix

Abbreviations xiv

1. Introduction... 1

    A Dual-Focus Analytic Approach 2

    Purpose of This Report 4

2. Damage and Needs 5

    Data for the Damage and Needs Assessment 5

    Review and Prioritization of Available Data Sources 6

    Limitations of This Assessment 8

    Connecting the Damage and Needs Assessment to Course of Action Development............................ 10

3. Building the Basis for the Recovery Plan for Puerto Rico 12

    Setting a Vision for Puerto Rico... 12

    Capital Investments and Strategic Initiatives 12

4. Courses of Action 15

    Establishing Courses of Action 15

    Describing and Analyzing Courses of Action 21

    Estimating Costs of Courses of Action.. 24

    Caveats for Comparing Courses of Action.. 30

5. Facilitating the Government of Puerto Rico's Development of the Recovery Plan 31

    Decision Support Tool... 31

    Portfolios of Courses of Action to Achieve Recovery Plan Objectives 33

    Decision Support Engagements... 41

    Refining the Final Recovery Plan.. 44

    Identifying Funding Sources 45

6. Summary and the Way Forward 47

Appendix A. Sources Used in Course of Action Development, by Sector................................... 49

Appendix B. Course of Action Descriptions 59

    Available for download at www.rand.org/t/RR2597

References... 60

Figures

Figure 1.1. Generalized Top-Down and Bottom-Up Process for Recovery Plan Development 3

Figure 5.1. Decision Support Tool Page Listing Courses of Action from the Water Sector 32

Figure 5.2. General Depiction of How Courses of Action Are Bundled into Portfolios That Address Strategic Objectives 34

Figure 5.3. Portfolio Overview (Courses of Action and Costs) Visualization in the Decision Support Tool, Showing the Portfolios for the Water Strategic Objective 42

Tables

Table 3.1. Capital Investments... 13
Table 3.2. Strategic Initiatives 14
Table 4.1. Sector-Specific Scope and Approaches for Course of Action Development 18
Table 4.2. Examples of Common Labor Costs 28
Table 5.1. Capital Investment Portfolios 36
Table 5.2. Strategic Initiative Portfolios 39

Summary

On September 19 and 20, 2017, Hurricane Maria caused widespread destruction across the U.S. Commonwealth of Puerto Rico. Making landfall just two weeks after Hurricane Irma, Maria—a strong Category 4 storm—significantly damaged local infrastructure and interrupted the provision of essential and nonessential services to the people of Puerto Rico. Attention has now turned to the commonwealth's long-term recovery needs. A supplemental appropriations bill, passed by Congress on February 8, 2018, required the governor of Puerto Rico, in coordination with the Federal Emergency Management Agency (FEMA), the U.S. Department of Treasury, the U.S. Department of Energy, and other federal agencies with responsibilities under the National Disaster Recovery Framework (U.S. Department of Homeland Security, 2016), to submit a report to Congress, within 180 days of enactment of the legislation, that describes Puerto Rico's 12- and 24-month economic and disaster recovery plan.

The government of Puerto Rico's recovery plan was published in August 2018 (Governor of Puerto Rico, 2018a), and it lays out the priorities, goals, and expected outcomes of the recovery effort in Puerto Rico. An overarching goal of the recovery plan is to mitigate vulnerabilities to future disasters and increase community resilience. The plan was designed to be consistent with Puerto Rico's fiscal capacity to operate and maintain rebuilt or replaced assets over the long term, and it will implement FEMA's Public Assistance Alternative Procedures Guide for Permanent Work (Section 428) in Puerto Rico (Pub. L. 113-2, 2013). FEMA asked the Homeland Security Operational Analysis Center (HSOAC) to provide analytical support to the government of Puerto Rico in its formulation of the recovery plan.[1]

This report summarizes the information gathering and analysis process that HSOAC used to support the government of Puerto Rico in its development of the recovery plan. The report describes how HSOAC produced a detailed damage and needs assessment (DNA) report and developed an array of potential courses of action (COAs) that Puerto Rico could pursue to repair damage from the hurricanes and address longer-term economic recovery needs (Fischbach et al., 2020). This report offers an overview of the core steps that HSOAC took to support plan development, explaining how the COAs were developed and how they were used in the plan development process, but this report does not address the specific COAs selected for the government of Puerto Rico's recovery plan.

---

[1] More information about HSOAC's contribution to planning for recovery in Puerto Rico, along with links to other reports being published as part of this series, can be found at www.rand.org/hsoac/puerto-rico-recovery.

A Dual-Focus Analytic Approach

HSOAC used a hybrid top-down and bottom-up process to develop the elements that would contribute to the recovery plan. The top-down process began by defining a vision for Puerto Rico, described at length in the recovery plan, *Transformation and Innovation in the Wake of Devastation: An Economic and Disaster Recovery Plan for Puerto Rico* (Government of Puerto Rico, 2018a). From this vision, 17 strategic objectives were developed to provide thematic aspirations to guide investments through portfolios and COAs. The bottom-up process was carried out by 12 teams of experts, organized by sector.[2] The bottom-up process began with the DNA, which informed the development of the COAs. HSOAC technical experts worked with relevant experts in the government of Puerto Rico, the federal government, and other key stakeholders to develop and analyze COAs and then, through a collaborative process with stakeholders, created portfolios of COAs, each of which focused on accomplishing a specific strategic objective. Decisionmakers and stakeholders then combined groups of portfolios, covering all strategic objectives, to determine which combination best represented the most desirable course forward for Puerto Rico. This final combination of portfolios formed the basis of the recovery plan submitted by the governor. This simultaneous top-down and bottom-up process supported continuous interactions and feedback between HSOAC team members and stakeholders, allowing them to adjust COAs and portfolios of COAs when, for example, choices made by Puerto Rico decisionmakers or additional information became available.

Damage and Needs Assessment

The DNA provides an overview of prehurricane conditions, hurricane damage, posthurricane conditions from the time of writing in spring 2018, and the remaining recovery needs in Puerto Rico (Fischbach et al., 2020). The DNA describes these damages and needs, as of spring 2018, by sector and by key issues and needs that have cross-sector relevance. Prehurricane conditions consist of trends, challenges, and other long-term stresses affecting Puerto Rico prior to the 2017 hurricanes; hurricane damage consists of direct damage to physical infrastructure from the 2017 hurricanes, as well as impacts to the economy, workforce, and population; posthurricane conditions describe the state of Puerto Rico as of spring 2018; and remaining needs consist of recovery and resilience issues not yet resolved as of spring 2018—this consists of both short-terms needs (that could be addressed within 12–24 months of the 2017 hurricane season) and longer-term needs (that could be addressed within ten years). The DNA also notes any key information gaps or missing data as of the writing of the document.

---

[2] The 12 designated sector teams are Water, Communications and Information Technology, Community Planning and Capacity Building, Municipalities, Economic, Energy, Housing, Transportation, Health and Social Services, Education, Natural and Cultural Resources, and Public Buildings. These sectors align with FEMA's organizational structure for the hurricane response.

Across all sectors, more than 100 data sources—with hundreds more individual data sets examined within those sources—were used for the assessment. The sources span all data types (qualitative, quantitative, primary, and secondary) and cover a variety of time periods (historical, baseline, immediately posthurricane, and posthurricane recovery). FEMA, other federal partners, and the government of Puerto Rico provided most of the data, in the form of both quantitative data sets and documents and qualitative data gathered through interviews and discussions with subject-matter experts. Other sources of information and analysis were municipal governments in Puerto Rico, literature reviews, interviews with key stakeholders, media reporting (to gather or cross-check data), and open-source data. In a few cases, HSOAC commissioned new primary-data collection. The HSOAC team also collaborated closely with FEMA's federal Recovery Support Functions, as well as with the government of Puerto Rico (e.g., the Central Recovery and Reconstruction Office) through briefings, workshops, meetings, and interim document reviews. The limitations of these data sources were numerous and are noted in the DNA.

Courses of Action

The COAs delineate potential activities, policies, programs, and strategies designed to further the goals prioritized by the government of Puerto Rico and other commonwealth stakeholders. Each individual COA describes an approach to addressing a problem or issue associated with hurricane damage or with a preexisting condition that inhibits economic recovery. To develop the COAs, the HSOAC team established 12 expert sector teams. These sector teams worked in varying degrees of partnership or consultation with FEMA's Recovery Support Function teams and field coordinators, FEMA sector teams, and local partners and stakeholders. The HSOAC team relied heavily on HSOAC and external (e.g., federal, local, and the government of Puerto Rico) experts to develop the COAs, and many COAs are adapted in part or in full from actions or investments defined by organizations other than HSOAC. Appendix A provides the sources that contributed to the COA development process, and Appendix B presents the resulting COAs, which are the building blocks that were analyzed, deliberated, and assembled as inputs to the long-term recovery plan development.

For each COA, the project team evaluated costs and put together a rough order-of-magnitude estimate, covering upfront costs and marginal increases to operations costs over a period of 11 years,[3] for carrying out the proposed action, activity, or program, including necessary investments. The precision of cost estimates varies widely across sectors: The scope of work in many COAs is broad and not always well suited for a detailed estimate. For this reason, some costs are reported as point estimates, while others are reported as ranges. The process of estimating costs, while aligned across sectors and COAs, necessarily depends on the nature of

---

[3] Costs were estimated for the 11-year period from fiscal years 2018 through 2028, which was the same time horizon of the certified new fiscal plan.

each COA, the information available to the team, and the time available to develop the cost estimate. The team also assessed the extent to which each COA embodies innovation and inclusiveness and is sensitive to future uncertainties or external factors. However, given the timeline for this work and the complexity of some benefit streams, the team did not calculate quantified or monetary benefits for the COAs. Despite these limitations, the cost information and limited outcome data were available to inform decisionmaking and prioritization.

Because of the diversity of stakeholder goals, there was no single dimension of merit or performance with which to analyze all the COAs. Instead, the HSOAC team identified four dimensions along which stakeholders could analyze, prioritize, and identify COAs that aligned with their goals:

- relevance of a COA to the strategic objectives
- alignment with attributes of innovation and inclusiveness established by the government of Puerto Rico
- sensitivity to a range of uncertainty categories
- cost.

The team did not estimate benefits for most COAs. Given the project constraints and the complex nature of many investments, the sector teams worked under the practical, but strong, assumption that COAs identified through the iterative, expert- and stakeholder-driven process would have positive net benefits. Indeed, ideas that did not pass a test of reasonableness were dropped during the COA development process.

Decision Support for the Government of Puerto Rico's Selection of Courses of Action for the Recovery Plan

To help the government of Puerto Rico select a cohesive and effective set of COAs for the recovery plan, the HSOAC team designed a decision framework and decision support tool (DST) to summarize and synthesize the possible COAs, inform the government of Puerto Rico's development and review of portfolios of COAs, and support engagement with the government of Puerto Rico and local officials who ultimately defined and selected portfolios for the recovery plan. The DST was designed for an iterative process: The project team assembled available information about possible COAs and groupings of COAs and then used the DST to engage government of Puerto Rico officials and collaborators to refine these inputs and elicit their preferences on an approach for recovery. Over multiple cycles and iterations of formal decision support engagements and informal sector meetings, this process helped HSOAC refine the specific COAs that are included in Puerto Rico's recovery plan.

The HSOAC team built portfolios of COAs for each strategic objective, in many cases with contributions from HSOAC experts and external subject-matter experts. This enabled the team to use expert judgment to factor in the damages and needs of the sectors, identify how multiple

COAs work together to achieve a strategic objective, and come to an understanding of precursors and interdependencies across sectors.

The government of Puerto Rico built the recovery plan based on portfolios that were informed by strategic objectives, through a series of engagements supported by the HSOAC team. The DST enabled users to review the portfolios and choose among them to define a possible recovery plan. The DST calculated the total cost of the plan and summarized the COAs included in the portfolios—this was important feedback for the portfolio selection process.

HSOAC's Interactive Engagement with the Government of Puerto Rico

The HSOAC team interacted closely with the government of Puerto Rico at all stages of the process. In addition to conducting the DNA and developing courses of action, the HSOAC team developed draft portfolios of COAs in collaboration with partners, held numerous engagements with the government of Puerto Rico to review and compare portfolios, developed new COAs when necessary, and updated portfolios to reflect government of Puerto Rico feedback. The government of Puerto Rico examined and compared these final portfolios and their respective solutions for each of their strategic objectives. Ultimately, the analysis and support provided by the HSOAC team facilitated the governor's final decision on which COAs and portfolios to select, but neither HSOAC nor the decision support engagements exclusively determined the content of the final recovery plan.

Abbreviations

CIT	Communications and Information Technology sector
COA	course of action
COR3	Central Office of Recovery, Reconstruction, and Resilience
CPCB	Community Planning and Capacity Building sector
DHS	U.S. Department of Homeland Security
DNA	damage and needs assessment
DST	decision support tool
ECN	Economic sector
EDU	Education sector
ENR	Energy sector
FEMA	Federal Emergency Management Agency
FOMB	Financial Oversight and Management Board
FTE	full-time equivalent
FY	fiscal year
GAR	governor's authorized representative
HOU	Housing sector
HSOAC	Homeland Security Operational Analysis Center
HSS	Health and Social Services sector
HUD	U.S. Department of Housing and Urban Development
MUN	Municipalities sector
NCR	Natural and Cultural Resources Sector
NDRF	National Disaster Recovery Framework
NGO	nongovernmental organization
O&M	operations and maintenance
PBD	Public Buildings sector
PRASA	Puerto Rico Aqueduct Sewer Authority
PRDOH	Puerto Rico Department of Housing
PREPA	Puerto Rico Electric Power Authority
PRIDCO	Puerto Rico Industrial Development Company
RSF	Recovery Support Function
TXN	Transportation sector
WTR	Water sector

1. Introduction

On September 19 and 20, 2017, Hurricane Maria caused widespread destruction across the U.S. Commonwealth of Puerto Rico. Making landfall just two weeks after Hurricane Irma, Maria—a strong Category 4 storm—significantly damaged local infrastructure and interrupted the provision of nonessential and essential services to the people of Puerto Rico. On September 20, 2017, President Donald Trump signed a major disaster declaration for Hurricane Maria (Federal Emergency Management Agency [FEMA], 2017) under the Robert T. Stafford Disaster Relief and Emergency Assistance Act (Stafford Act; Pub. L. 100-707, 1988).

When the hurricanes struck, Puerto Rico had been grappling with an economic crisis for more than a decade. Structural changes in demography, social stresses, deterioration of infrastructure, weak government accountability, and significant numbers of people leaving Puerto Rico combined to exacerbate the impact of the hurricanes. Transformative changes and substantial investments in the years to come will be necessary to cope with both new and long-standing challenges facing Puerto Rico.

On February 8, 2018, in response to the damage wrought in Puerto Rico by Hurricanes Irma and Maria, Congress passed the Further Additional Supplemental Appropriations for Disaster Relief Requirements Act, 2018 (a portion of Pub. L. 115-123, 2018). This act required the governor of Puerto Rico (Ricardo Rosselló Nevares), in coordination with FEMA, the U.S. Department of Treasury, the U.S. Department of Energy, and other federal agencies with responsibilities under the National Disaster Recovery Framework (NDRF; see U.S. Department of Homeland Security [DHS], 2016) to submit a report to Congress, within 180 days, that describes Puerto Rico's 12- and 24-month economic and disaster recovery plan. The act mandated that the recovery plan define "the priorities, goals, and expected outcomes of the recovery effort for the Commonwealth based on damage assessments prepared pursuant to Federal law, if applicable," for the following sectors: housing, economic issues, health and social services, natural and cultural resources, governance and civic institutions, electric power systems and grid restoration, environmental issues, and other infrastructure systems. The recovery plan is intended to provide Puerto Rico a path toward economic sustainability, growth, and resilience as it reconstructs and recovers from the impact of Hurricanes Irma and Maria. FEMA asked the Homeland Security Operational Analysis Center (HSOAC) to develop an information base that would inform the development of the plan by the government of Puerto Rico. This report summarizes the information gathering and analysis process that HSOAC used to support the government of Puerto Rico in its development of the recovery plan.

The HSOAC team solicited feedback from external subject-matter experts and stakeholders in Puerto Rico, assessed damage and recovery needs by sector, clarified priorities, identified and evaluated potential solutions, and estimated rough order-of-magnitude costs, as well as identified funding mechanisms, for an array of courses of action (COAs), which are recovery activities designed to redress the hurricane damages and preexisting economic needs that Puerto Rico faces. This iterative and collaborative planning process provided the basis for developing the recovery plan, with the final decisions on the content of the plan made by the Governor of Puerto Rico, not HSOAC. This report is intended to give the reader insight into the methodology behind the recovery planning process.

A Dual-Focus Analytic Approach

HSOAC took a dual top-down and bottom-up approach to gathering information and forming inputs to the recovery plan, an approach informed by formal strategic planning processes. Planning processes implemented by the government often use a top-down approach. The U.S. Department of Defense's processes for long-term and crisis action planning and FEMA's process for disaster and emergency incident management are examples of top-down approaches (Joint Chiefs of Staff, 2017; FEMA, 2014, 2015). Top-down processes begin with strategic guidance from informed, broadly experienced executives or executive bodies, and then proceed through successively more detailed and focused planning activities to identify specific initiatives that specialized personnel can implement to achieve stated objectives. Top-down planning processes are typically not driven by any single event or condition, but instead are intended to support a strategy applicable to many situations that may emerge.

By contrast, bottom-up planning is often deployed in response to a specific event or condition. The NDRF is an example of a bottom-up approach (DHS, 2016). The NDRF provides a framework that identifies postdisaster needs and damage, and it then develops recovery processes to meet those needs and respond to the damage directly. The advantage of bottom-up planning is that observed needs (e.g., hurricane damage or other underlying needs) can directly drive the generation of possible solutions. A bottom-up approach also focuses attention on the specific investments and initiatives required to achieve a broader goal or objective.

Both of these planning approaches present challenges when used in the context of disaster recovery. For example, top-down planning may require considerable time and resources to tailor strategic initiatives to a real-world disaster setting, lengthening the recovery planning process or compromising plan applicability. With bottom-up planning, observed needs can vary in their scope and complexity; as a result, solutions and actions generated from the bottom up may also vary in scope and complexity. Both top-down and bottom-up planning require a systematic approach to valuing and choosing among potential recovery solutions and actions.

Given the extent and severity of hurricane damage in Puerto Rico, the need for a rapid shift from *planning* to *executing* the recovery plan was significant. HSOAC, in concert with FEMA and the government of Puerto Rico, implemented a collaborative planning process that was simultaneously top-down and bottom-up: The goal was to link observed needs most efficiently with investments that would put Puerto Rico on a path toward recovery shaped by the government of Puerto Rico's identified strategic objectives. The combined top-down and bottom-up planning process was implemented collaboratively with the government of Puerto Rico's Central Office of Recovery, Reconstruction, and Resilience (COR3), FEMA sector teams, FEMA Recovery Support Function (RSF) teams, and RSF field coordinators, with some input from the Office of the Chief Innovation Officer of Puerto Rico and other agencies in the government of Puerto Rico. This collaborative process helped guide planning for the substantial investments necessary to support Puerto Rico's rebuilding effort. This approach is based on best practices for integrating analysis into planning deliberation processes, as recommended by the National Research Council (National Research Council, 2009).

The HSOAC team customized this top-down, bottom-up approach to incorporate both the detailed analysis of damages and needs and the COAs, assembled by the teams of experts, organized into 12 sectors, within a decision analysis framework. This process entailed assembling groups of COAs into alternative portfolios to enable the government of Puerto Rico and stakeholders to weigh different approaches to recovery (portfolios are explained in detail in Chapter 5). A decision support tool (DST) then helped stakeholders select one portfolio for each strategic objective. Figure 1.1 depicts this general process, although the details and timeline within each step were different for some sectors.

Figure 1.1. Generalized Top-Down and Bottom-Up Process for Recovery Plan Development

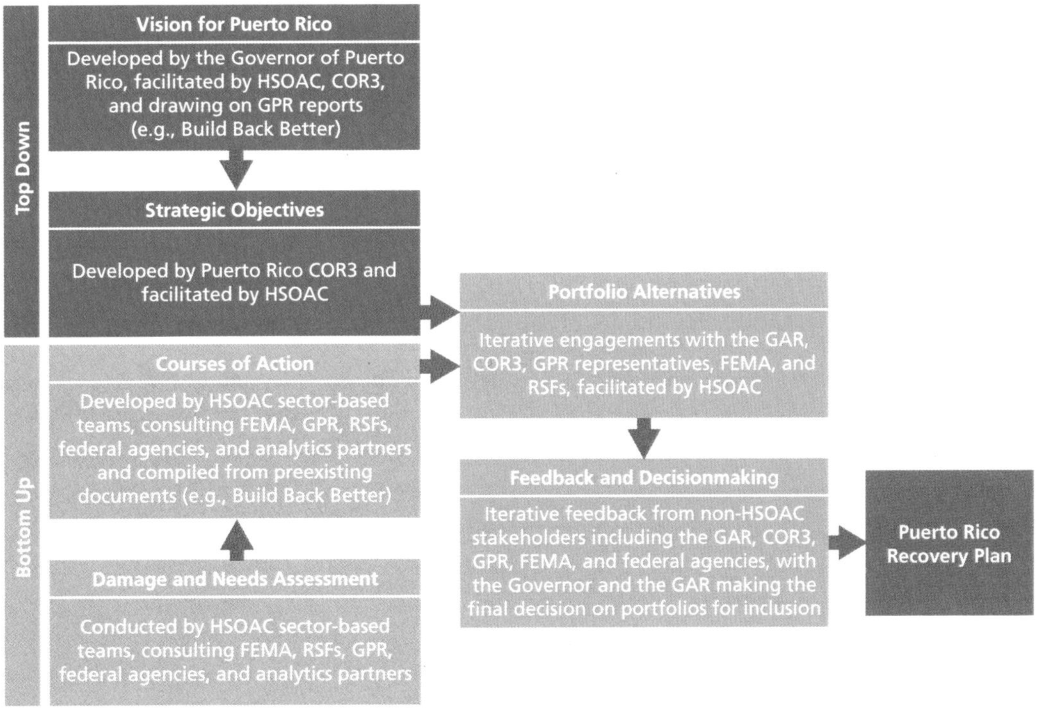

NOTES: GPR = government of Puerto Rico; GAR = Governor's Authorized Representative (the GAR was appointed to the COR3 by the governor in February 2018 to be the state leader in the Hurricane Maria recovery effort, reporting to the governor directly). For the *Build Back Better* report, see Governor of Puerto Rico, 2017.

Purpose of This Report

This report summarizes the strategic planning process that HSOAC used to support the government of Puerto Rico in its development of a recovery plan for Puerto Rico. The recovery plan, *Transformation and Innovation in the Wake of Devastation: An Economic and Disaster Recovery Plan for Puerto Rico* (Government of Puerto Rico, 2018a), presents the government of Puerto Rico's vision and priorities for capital investments and strategic initiatives. This report describes HSOAC's approach to conducting the DNA, developing COAs, and creating portfolios of COAs,[4] all with input from and engagement with partners and stakeholders. This report also highlights additional features of the COA development process, including the COA attributes that were relevant to the government of Puerto Rico's decisionmaking process. Accompanying reports provide additional details on the DNA and on sector-specific analyses, including descriptions of the specific COAs prioritized and selected for Puerto Rico's recovery plan.

---

[4] Appendix B presents all possible COAs and is available for download at www.rand.org/t/RR2597.

2. Damage and Needs

To determine the specific investments necessary to ensure a robust recovery in Puerto Rico, and in response to the requirements established by Congress in the supplemental appropriations bill, HSOAC developed a DNA report, *After Hurricane Maria: Predisaster Conditions, Hurricane Damage, and Recovery Needs in Puerto Rico* (Fischbach et al., 2020). That assessment, which describes hurricane damage and remaining needs across Puerto Rico sector by sector and across sectors as of spring 2018, became the basis for defining, comparing, and prioritizing COAs. This chapter presents an overview of the DNA process, which relied largely on secondary federal and commonwealth data and limited primary data collection. This chapter also discusses how the DNA findings for each sector influenced the development of the COAs.

Data for the Damage and Needs Assessment

HSOAC sector teams conducted damage and needs assessments between February and June 2018, using a sector team organization and a damage assessment process that aligned with the federal posthurricane NDRF process. Across all 12 sectors, more than 100 primary and secondary data sources—with hundreds more individual data sets examined within those sources—were used to assess the condition of Puerto Rico prior to the storms, the damage inflicted by the storms, and the current needs facing the commonwealth. The data sources span data types (qualitative, quantitative, primary, secondary) and cover a variety of time periods (historical, baseline, immediately poststorm, poststorm recovery).

FEMA, other federal partners, the government of Puerto Rico, and municipal governments across the commonwealth provided the majority of data, in the form of both quantitative data sets and documents and qualitative data gathered through interviews, focus groups, and discussions with subject-matter experts. Some primary data were collected using the same methods by HSOAC sector teams. Other sources of data and analysis were literature reviews; interviews with subject-matter experts and key stakeholders; media reporting (to gather or cross-check data); and open-source data available through a variety of platforms, including U.S. federal government websites (e.g., U.S. Census Bureau), government of Puerto Rico websites, foundations that have worked in Puerto Rico, and OpenStreetMap. The team also collaborated closely with the RSFs for related sectors, as well as with members of the government of Puerto Rico, through briefings, workshops, meetings, and interim document reviews. Some data sets were particularly important to assessing damage—for example, FEMA individual assistance and public assistance requests, Community Conditions Assessment findings, and data sets provided by the U.S. Army Corps of Engineers and the U.S. Department of Housing and Urban Development (HUD). These agencies all have guidelines for determining and categorizing damage following a disaster and for quantifying recovery needs.

The specific data sources and methods used to assess damage and needs varied widely by sector. The DNA report more fully describes the data and methodologies used by each sector, including key data sources and methodologies applied to assess pre- or poststorm conditions and estimate hurricane impacts.

Review and Prioritization of Available Data Sources

Data Collection and Screening

The initial step in the damage assessment process involved outreach to FEMA, other federal agencies, government of Puerto Rico agencies, and nongovernmental stakeholders to help build understanding of the institutional arrangements and responsibilities for recovery and to survey potential sources of information on damage in each sector. Sector teams sought data that would help them understand historical context and background; prestorm conditions, trends, and challenges; hurricane damage; and poststorm conditions, including emergency response, repairs made to date, and remaining needs. To determine the breadth and depth of available data, sectors made it a priority to identify damage assessments—or proposals for ongoing assessments—being conducted by all stakeholders in Puerto Rico. Data sources were identified primarily through open-source public information, discussions with subject-matter experts and stakeholders, and information gathered through FEMA working group meetings attended by the HSOAC sector teams. In this early stage, HSOAC sector teams also reviewed literature on assessments to develop specific aspects of the damage assessment for the Puerto Rico context.

HSOAC screened all the data collected and received for relevance and combined or summarized as needed. Once relevant data sources were identified, the HSOAC team sought access to those data through RSFs, FEMA's sector chiefs and deputy chiefs, government of Puerto Rico agencies or departments, and other entities as appropriate and as available. The HSOAC team also identified data resources that were likely to become available in the future and asked subcontractors to obtain other key information through intensive data collection efforts.

Qualitative data analysis gathered from conversations with stakeholders and experts, and also from the literature, was supplemented with quantitative data analyses whenever possible. Many sectors also reviewed media reports to gather qualitative data for analysis or to help prioritize other data-gathering activities. Although of varying depth, coverage, and reliability, taken together these accounts offer an overview of popular and official opinion regarding the damage inflicted by the hurricanes on different population groups and localities. These accounts also explain the posthurricane needs of and assistance provided to population groups and localities in the response and recovery periods. Disaster and communication researchers frequently turn to this type of content analysis to examine agenda settings (Barnes et al., 2008), disaster frames (Tierney, Bevc, and Kuligowski, 2006), responses from authorities (Littlefield and Quenette, 2007), and audiences' media needs during disasters (Houston et al., 2015). Accordingly, many of the HSOAC sector teams used content analysis to better understand the impact, response, and recovery from Hurricanes Irma and Maria in Puerto Rico.

Depending on the availability of data early in the process, sector teams took a variety of approaches to reviewing and prioritizing data sources based on relevancy, comprehensiveness, and credibility: Most started with qualitative, firsthand information, while others began with secondary, quantitative data sets.[5] Sector teams that began with qualitative data conducted interviews with critical stakeholders and subject-matter experts and performed document reviews to get a better understanding of the type of data available for a sector. Qualitative analysis of these data helped teams assess the accuracy and completeness of sources and prioritize quantitative data for analysis as they became available. Sector teams that began with quantitative data sets, such as publicly available government data or geospatial data, examined the data to understand the extent of the information available (particularly at baseline) and to identify remaining critical information gaps. This approach helped them obtain a broad perspective across the whole of Puerto Rico about general pre- and poststorm conditions, and it allowed them to prioritize more in-depth data collection. This approach also facilitated discussions about recovery goals and needs.

When multiple damage assessments existed for a particular service or asset (e.g., single-family homes), sector teams reviewed them for comprehensiveness and cross-checked them for consistency. Where data disagreed, the approach was either to resolve the difference or present both sets of information. Existing damage assessments were not always standardized, and they rarely provided cost estimates. Data analysis often focused on consolidating several different damage or status surveys into a single consistent system assessment. When damage data were not available on particular services or assets, sectors used proxy information when possible, with the goal of replacing it with more-detailed data; in some extreme cases, they used a representative sample of data or qualitative data.

In some instances, sector teams developed their own data collection tools, such as surveys, focus groups (particularly with populations disproportionately affected by the hurricanes), and interviews with subject-matter experts and key stakeholders. Two sector teams—Municipalities and Community Planning and Capacity Building—held roundtables and workshops, respectively, which drew from the public, municipalities, and mayors for data and input. For some sectors, subcontractors conducted the initial analyses, with support from other subcontractors and HSOAC as necessary. The HSOAC team then combined these analyses of the primary qualitative data collected with other data to generate final outputs.

---

[5] The sector-specific reports provide more information about how each sector approached this and other research and analysis steps.

Data Analysis

Initial analyses were largely descriptive and included baseline summaries about prestorm conditions; later analyses were more sophisticated when the data allowed. Most sectors relied on at least some data sources that had already been analyzed by external researchers. In these cases, reviewing the data for accuracy, uncertainties, assumptions, and gaps helped to determine whether and what supplemental data collection was warranted. The teams made every attempt to assemble the most-comprehensive information possible; teams leveraged all available data to avoid duplication of prior data requests and limit the burden on stakeholders and partners.

The teams analyzed different types of data (qualitative and quantitative, primary and secondary) in different ways. Analysis across most sectors occurred at the same time as data collection, with data collection topics evolving as the study progressed. Comparisons were made between groups, geographic regions, and data sources (e.g., comparisons to the continental United States, rural versus urban communities). Some data were also collected for different time periods (e.g., before the hurricane, and week by week after); we compared these data to develop a longitudinal understanding of the disaster and recovery process.

Most qualitative data were analyzed using Dedoose, a qualitative data analysis software.[6] Sector teams used Dedoose to analyze the primary data collected from interviews and focus groups led by HSOAC and partner organizations, including the University of Puerto Rico and the International City/County Management Association. Transcripts were coded for common themes using deductive codes derived from the literature and inductive codes developed as data analysis proceeded.

Limitations of This Assessment

Working in Puerto Rico in the postdisaster recovery environment was challenging, not least because of data and capacity issues that preceded the 2017 hurricanes. The primary challenge to comprehensive damage assessment was data gaps which remained at the time the DNA report was published. For example, the report was limited by a lack of systematic data collection in many sectors before the assessment effort (e.g., damage assessments for different habitats in the Natural and Cultural Resources sector) and by data lags during the assessment effort (e.g., economic impacts). In addition, data collection was sometimes hindered when ownership of data within sectors was unclear. It is also worth noting that the pace at which recovery activities were proceeding and the influx of recovery capacity across Puerto Rico were in and of themselves barriers to systematic data collection and timely communication.

---

[6] The software is available at www.dedoose.com.

Key Data Gaps

After gathering and reviewing data sources and conducting preliminary analyses, each sector team identified remaining data gaps. Given the decentralized nature of many services and assets in Puerto Rico, sectors identified many data gaps around poststorm conditions, status, and functioning. Obtaining sufficient data to assess the secondary effects of damage (e.g., health ramifications of diesel as a power source, water-borne illness from poor water quality) was also often a challenge for sectors.

The first critical gap, particularly for the Housing and Economic sectors, was the availability of data on "informal" housing construction and jobs, both of which were prevalent in Puerto Rico even before the 2017 hurricane season.[7] Estimates of the impact of informal construction and jobs were based on the literature and on data from the formal components of these sectors. Because there is no record of informal transactions, accurate data may never be available and the likelihood of a truly comprehensive assessment of the damage and needs in these sectors is limited.

In addition, the HSOAC team did not have access to detailed information about the needs of, and the assistance provided to, potentially marginalized populations in the aftermath of Hurricanes Irma and Maria. Marginalized populations traditionally include older people, women, children, disabled people, undocumented people, and people living in informal housing. These populations may be more vulnerable than the general population because of their preexisting risk factors.

A second critical gap was caused by the limitations of using private-sector and For Official Use Only (FOUO) data. For example, the Communications and Information Technology sector was able to obtain data from the private sector but was not able to use these data for the DNA because they were proprietary. If information from these sources was included, it was presented at an aggregate level rather than a granular or municipal level. As a result, this kind of sensitive information was not included in numerous sector data analyses. Similar issues existed for the Energy, Water, and Health and Social Services sectors.

A third critical gap was in the infeasibility of collecting data from all possible data stewards within a sector. Subsequently, some sectors relied on data from a few providers to represent the overall state of the sector. For example, the Public Buildings sector relied primarily on data from the Puerto Rico Industrial Development Company (PRIDCO) and the Puerto Rico Public Buildings Authority because data could not feasibly be collected from the many other owners of public buildings. Similar issues existed for the Municipalities, Natural and Cultural Resources, and Health and Social Services sectors.

Finally, the estimated damage costs presented in the DNA should be interpreted with caution because they represent a best guess at the time of writing. The approach to estimating the

---

[7] *Informal* implies housing constructed without proper permits or work being conducted "off the books."

damage costs to a given asset was based on the asset's specific nature and the available sources of information robust enough to inform the estimate. There were also limitations to using individual assistance and public assistance requests to estimate costs, since these estimates are based on costs to bring structures into a "habitable state," rather than a state of improved condition or resilience. The quality and availability of information varied by and within sectors, so some damage estimates were much more precise than others. Damage information presented in the DNA report should be regarded as preliminary, since more-specific cost estimates will depend on how recovery options will be implemented and how ongoing damage assessments are completed.

Methods Applied to Address Data Gaps

Sector teams often used a mixed-methods approach to address data gaps. Some sectors relied on discussions, interviews, and meetings with key stakeholders, such as local contacts in Puerto Rico (e.g., universities, government of Puerto Rico departments and agencies, FEMA, nongovernmental organizations [NGOs], and mayors). Others used open-source information, such as websites, documents, and media reports. Sectors also used analytical techniques to calculate approximate outputs when uncertainty existed and when validation was not possible.

In some cases, when data were incomplete or missing, the HSOAC sector teams made estimates using analogies with similar assets with more-complete data. For example, available estimates of damage to a particular type of water facility (e.g., a wastewater treatment plan) were applied to other facilities of the same type that lacked assessments. In other cases, uncertainty was quantified by identifying ranges of outputs for analysis where multiple conflicting data sets existed and where validation was not possible. The death count, for example, remained disputed by different sources until June 2018, when the governor-commissioned study by the Milken Institute School of Public Health at George Washington University released its official count of 2,975 excess deaths (Milken Institute School of Public Health, George Washington University, 2018). To the extent possible, available estimates in a given region were applied in an effort to account for spatial variation. This approach was intended to provide an initial rough order-of-magnitude estimate of the entirety of the damage in each sector.

Connecting the Damage and Needs Assessment to Course of Action Development

Ultimately, the process of describing, sector by sector, the prestorm conditions and the specific storm impacts and damage was also a means of identifying critical needs to address with the recovery plan. The areas in need of investment, including through COAs developed to support the recovery plan, include the following:

- **prehurricane conditions:** recent trends, challenges, or other long-term stresses affecting Puerto Rico before Hurricanes Irma and Maria

10

- **damage:** damage caused by Hurricanes Irma and Maria—includes direct damage to infrastructure or capital, as well as effects on Puerto Rico's economy, workforce, municipal governments, and population during and in the aftermath of hurricane season (through spring 2018)[8]
- **posthurricane conditions:** status of various sectors following emergency response and early recovery investments, as of spring 2018 (March to May, depending on sector)
- **remaining needs:** remaining needs to address during hurricane recovery not resolved as of spring 2018, drawing from both pre–Irma and Maria conditions and hurricane damage.

The DNA provided a critical rationale and baseline for developing COAs that the governor selected as the key investments to achieve the government of Puerto Rico's goals and vision. The DNA report was also a reference tool throughout the later stages of the recovery planning process for the HSOAC sector teams and other federal and local partners.

---

[8] The cutoff date for information varies across sectors but was no earlier than March 2018.

3. Building the Basis for the Recovery Plan for Puerto Rico

Although the DNA report (Fischbach et al., 2020) identified needs to be addressed, the recovery plan (Governor of Puerto Rico, 2018a) is intended to guide investments to meet these needs and thereby propel Puerto Rico toward a broader transformational vision of social and economic progress. As the HSOAC team was assembling the DNA report, the government of Puerto Rico was developing and articulating its vision, goals, and strategic objectives for recovery.

Setting a Vision for Puerto Rico

HSOAC team members worked alongside the Governor's Office and COR3 to establish a vision for Puerto Rico. The following steps guided this effort (Government of Puerto Rico, 2018):

- defining what recovery means for Puerto Rico
- establishing principles for how the government of Puerto Rico, NGOs, private organizations, and nonprofit agencies should work together toward recovery
- describing phases through which recovery should progress
- identifying the most-pressing recovery issues and the priority actions, potential partners, and resources needed to address each recovery issue
- committing to measuring and reporting on progress toward recovery

The governor's recovery planning focused on four primary goals: (1) ensuring that rebuilding and restoration efforts promote sustainable economic growth and social transformation; (2) promoting an educated, healthy, and sustainable society; (3) optimizing Puerto Rico's critical infrastructure by rethinking its design and reconstruction; and (4) enhancing Puerto Rico's ability to withstand and recover from future disasters. These goals reflect not only Puerto Rico's most-pressing recovery needs but also what the government of Puerto Rico believes is the best path forward to ensure that Puerto Rico rebuilds both for today and the future.

Capital Investments and Strategic Initiatives

The government of Puerto Rico began by defining 17 strategic objectives that collectively reflected the vision for rebuilding Puerto Rico. These objectives were divided into nine capital investment categories and eight strategic initiatives (see Tables 3.1 and 3.2). This investment framework distinguishes between foundational capital investments, which provide the critical base for Puerto Rico's recovery, and strategic initiatives, which, through investment and policies, aim to achieve a particular economic or social outcome.

The focus of the capital investments (Table 3.1) is on repairing and improving the physical infrastructure and other natural and social structures in Puerto Rico. The government of Puerto Rico saw these investments as foundational to many other recovery activities and as a way to establish the environment for economic development and growth.

The strategic initiatives (Table 3.2) reflect the government of Puerto Rico's preferred approach for leveraging and enhancing Puerto Rico's strengths to yield a robust economy and a resilient and healthy society for the future. In other words, these strategic initiatives were based on visionary ideals designed to transform Puerto Rico. For example, the strategic initiative for entrepreneurship was designed to expand entrepreneurial opportunities and contribute to economic development.

Table 3.1. Capital Investments

Sector	Description
Energy	**Transform the energy system:** customer-centric, affordable, reliable, and scalable electricity that incorporates more renewables, microgrids, and distributed energy resources and can drive new businesses and employment opportunities and support residents' well-being
Transportation	**Rebuild and strengthen maritime, surface, and air transportation:** a flexible and reliable transportation system that moves people and goods to ensure economic continuity and facilitate disaster response
Water	**Rethink water systems:** safe and reliable water systems that are protected from future disasters to ensure the well-being of the people of Puerto Rico and the operations of government and businesses
Communications and Information Technology	**Modernize the telecommunications system:** fast, reliable, and resilient residential, commercial, and emergency communications that drive Puerto Rico's economy, prosperity, and well-being
Public Buildings	**Repair, rebuild, and rightsize the inventory of public buildings:** stronger and more-resilient public buildings that meet today's standards, mitigate against future disasters, represent innovative designs, and meet communities' needs
Housing	**Repair and rebuild resilient residential housing:** safe, secure, and affordable residential housing to create a better built environment
Education	**Transform the education system:** competitive graduates with knowledge and skills needed to adapt to changes in the economy, environment, and technology
Health and Social Services	**Rebuild and enhance health and social service infrastructure and regional health care networks:** reliable and equitable access to health and social services and health-promoting communities, including an efficient and effective response to public health crises and other future disasters
Natural and Cultural Resources	**Restore, plan, and develop the natural environment:** marine and terrestrial ecosystems that coexist sustainability with tourism and economic development of Puerto Rico and protect against storm damage

Table 3.2. Strategic Initiatives

Initiative	Description
Ocean Economy (BLUEtide)	Integrate and promote all of Puerto Rico's ocean-dependent industries and ecosystems as a cohesive effort to promote economic growth and improve quality of life for residents and enhance the visitor experience
Visitor Economy	Develop a strong visitor economy to help position Puerto Rico as a global destination of investment, production, and wealth
Digital Transformation	Build digital capabilities and workforce needed to fundamentally transform key industry and government processes, making them more user-focused, relevant, and efficient at addressing local needs and delivering basic services
Entrepreneurship	Expand opportunities for entrepreneurship and development of small to medium-size local business that can compete globally to promote economic development
Advanced Manufacturing	Address policy and structural barriers to increase opportunities for investment and the growth of private-public partnerships
Agricultural Modernization and Processing	Optimize agriculture to promote greater productivity and output and improve exports
Emergency Services Modernization and Integration	Enhance public safety and first responders' ability to deliver reliable, integrated emergency services
Twenty-First Century Workforce	Develop and protect human capital to establish a world-class workforce, increase labor force flexibility, and create high-quality employment opportunities aligned with economic growth strategies

4. Courses of Action

In this effort, we used the term *course of action* as the descriptor of the recovery actions developed to address the pre- and posthurricane damage and needs uncovered in this research. The COAs described in this chapter delineate potential activities, policies, programs, and strategies designed to achieve the vision and goals prioritized by the government of Puerto Rico and other commonwealth stakeholders. Consistent with Figure 1.1, COAs are the starting point of the bottom-up process for recovery planning. This chapter describes how COAs were developed and how they can be analyzed and compared.

Establishing Courses of Action

To develop the COAs, HSOAC formed expert teams across 12 sectors, referred to as *sector teams*. These sector teams worked in varying degrees of partnership or consultation with sector RSFs, FEMA sector teams, the government of Puerto Rico, municipalities, and local partners and stakeholders. The 12 sectors were designed to mimic the coordinating structure that FEMA employs for disaster response, which includes teams for housing, community planning and capacity building, health and social services, economics, natural and cultural resources, and infrastructure systems. For the response to Hurricane Maria, specifically, FEMA divided the infrastructure systems and health and social services teams into separate sectors (e.g., the social services team divided into the health and social services sector and the education sector) and added a municipalities team. In response, HSOAC created 12 COA sector teams: Communications and Information Technology, Community Planning and Capacity Building, Economic, Education, Energy,[9] Health and Social Services, Housing, Municipalities, Natural and Cultural Resources, Public Buildings, Transportation, and Water. An HSOAC cross-sector integration team was also established to help create pathways of communication and coordination among the individual sector teams.

The recovery challenges and opportunities facing each sector team were distinct and diverse, and each sector team took an approach to developing COAs that reflected the diversity of challenges while balancing the need for methodological consistency across teams. The resulting COAs are presented in Appendix B (available for download at www.rand.org/t/RR2597). The COAs are the product of sector-level, bottom-up inputs, and they are meant to be analyzed, deliberated over, and implemented in combination to meet the goals and vision of the recovery plan defined from the top down by the government of Puerto Rico.

---

[9] Although FEMA had the Power sector, the HSOAC team maintained the corresponding Energy sector to mimic the broader purview of the RSF.

Defining Courses of Action

Other organizations have used the term *COA* to describe generally an action to be taken toward some goal or desired outcome:

- FEMA defines a *COA* as "a scheme that explains how an operation can be accomplished, and what resources may be required. The purpose of COAs is to provide senior leadership with options, and it is the responsibility of the planning team to develop, evaluate, and recommend viable options. A fully developed COA explains who does what and when to achieve the desired outcome. It identifies the resources, capabilities, and information requirements to carry out the strategy" (FEMA, 2014, p. 53).
- The U.S. Joint Chiefs of Staff defines a *COA* as "a potential way (solution, method) to accomplish the assigned mission. The staff develop COAs to provide unique options to the commander, all oriented on accomplishing the military end state. A good COA accomplishes the mission within the commander's guidance, provides flexibility to meet unforeseen events during execution, and positions the joint force for future operations. It also gives components the maximum latitude for initiative" (Joint Chiefs of Staff, 2017, p. 20).

These examples illustrate how COAs can contain significant detail (as in the FEMA definition) or consist of a broader path forward (as in the Joint Chiefs of Staff definition). The COAs that HSOAC developed for the Puerto Rico recovery planning effort take the middle ground: In some cases they describe an approach to a problem or issue associated with hurricane damage or a preexisting condition that inhibits economic recovery or economic growth; in other cases they address the larger context in which the problem or issue resides. In other words, a COA might prescribe a specific action that needs to be taken, such as extending a road, or it might describe a change in governance, operations, fiscal health, or capacity building that would enable solving the problem or improving the issue. COAs developed for the Puerto Rico disaster recovery need to support a range of recovery-relevant decisions across the 12 diverse sectors—and often also at multiple levels (e.g., federal, commonwealth, regional, local), since different decisions can be made at each level.

Many frameworks in peer-reviewed and other literature offer ways to systematically conceptualize problems, potential solutions, and feasible approaches to evaluating and choosing among potential COAs (e.g., a decision uncertainty screening tool [Moser, 2012], robust decision making [Lempert et al., 2013], assumption-based planning [Dewar, 2002]). These approaches all follow the National Research Council's recommendation for "deliberation with analysis," in which analysis does not provide a single solution—in this case, an optimal recovery plan—but instead supports deliberations over key trade-offs (National Research Council, 2009; Groves et al., 2014). Although the type and detail of input required, or deemed acceptable, at various stages in the decisionmaking process may vary, it was important to ensure that our approach to developing COAs aligned across sectors, especially when addressing trade-off questions that needed to balance multiple management strategies for multiple objectives; enhanced transparency and awareness; and allowed us to fine-tune and integrate our research methods and products coherently (Moser, 2012; Lempert et al., 2013; Dewar, 2002). However, given the complexity and speed of the recovery planning effort in Puerto Rico, it was also important to be flexible in our approach. For example, in Chapter 5, we discuss how, by design, the portfolio development process, which took place after the initial development of COAs, resulted in the addition of new COAs to fill gaps or address interdependencies within sectors.

For each COA, the HSOAC team identified the problem or issue the COA addresses, who might implement it, where and how it might be implemented, the estimated cost of implementation, potential or known funding options, and potential benefits, spillover effects, and pitfalls associated with the COA. Together, these characteristics describe each COA in a way that includes core information about what a COA is and what it does while balancing the need for COAs to be easily and quickly understood. COA information reflected the analysis the team compiled or conducted and was designed to support decisionmaking and further manipulation of COAs. The COA summaries were used for the DST and gave high-level decisionmakers and the general reader an idea of the proposed COAs, what each does, and how they may fit together.

The HSOAC team also created an expanded COA "justification"[10] with information that can help with more-precise planning for implementation. A COA-specific justification could also include supporting literature, examples from other parts of the world that set precedent for a COA, and sometimes more explicitly demarcated costs.

Although the COAs all share elements, they also differ in their respective levels of granularity, depending on the scope and complexity of a problem or issue, or the data or information available. Some COAs offer a stand-alone solution to meet a specific need, while others may be part of bundle of COAs that work in concert to achieve a broader goal. Because of time and complexity constraints, most COAs do not include quantified estimates of economic or other social benefits, although cost-benefit thinking was an implicit part of the COA vetting process.

Developing Courses of Action

Sector teams engaged in multiple activities to inform the COA development process, beginning with understanding the needs identified in the DNA. The teams conducted background research; engaged with sector stakeholders and subject-matter experts in Puerto Rico; and reviewed existing plans, proposals, and the literature to identify strategies, best practices, and possible innovations to meet those needs. Sector stakeholders and subject-matter experts were from federal and commonwealth government agencies, nonprofit organizations, NGOs, academics, private-sector operators and service providers, and professional associations. Sector teams also drew heavily from discussions held in larger sector-specific working groups and task

---

[10] The Energy and Economic sectors did not produce COA justifications because of the scale and complexity of COAs in those sectors and the time available. As a result, COAs for these sectors are presented only in the abridged summary format. For more detail, see the respective, separately published sector reports.

forces, and COAs were often formulated in partnership with FEMA RSF solutions-based teams, whose members consisted of FEMA sector experts, RSFs, and other topical experts and stakeholders. The solutions-based teams contributed practical knowledge, experience with relevant programs, and a deep understanding of the federal system. Internal and external peer reviewers, including those with expertise in disaster response and recovery, reviewed the COAs.[11]

The COAs were derived from a wide variety of sources, and they were informed by both subject-matter expertise and the needs identified through the DNA. Appendix A provides a list of these sources organized by sector. Sources used across all sectors were the *Build Back Better Puerto Rico* plan (Governor of Puerto Rico, 2017), the certified *New Fiscal Plan for Puerto Rico* (Government of Puerto Rico, 2018), and the *Reimagine Puerto Rico* report (Resilient Puerto Rico Advisory Commission, 2018).[12] The *Build Back Better Puerto Rico* plan was written by the Governor's Office in direct response to, and within weeks of, Hurricanes Irma and Maria. The certified *New Fiscal Plan for Puerto Rico* is a multiyear fiscal turnaround plan approved in 2018 by the Financial Oversight and Management Board (FOMB), a White House–appointed board established under the Puerto Rico Oversight, Management, and Economic Stability Act (PROMESA) (Pub. L. 114-187, 2016) to oversee the restructuring of Puerto Rico's debt. The approach to developing COAs used by each sector varied, and Table 4.1 provides brief summaries of the sector-specific approaches and scope. The table also highlights the sources and methods that each sector team used.

Table 4.1. Sector-Specific Scope and Approaches for Course of Action Development

Sector	Methodology
Communications and Information Technology	The Communications and Information Technology sector team engaged many partners and other organizations for its COA development. A team member was "embedded" in the FEMA Telecommunications/Information Technology sector during three weeks of daily brainstorming sessions and reviewed findings from the sector. In meetings with government of Puerto Rico officials across multiple agencies, such as the Puerto Rico Telecommunications Regulatory Board, the Office of the Chief Innovation Officer, the Department of Public Safety, and the Office of the Chief Information Officer, the team gathered critical context to ensure the feasibility and operational utility of COAs. These discussions, along with key documents, such as the *Build Back Better Puerto Rico* plan (Governor of Puerto Rico, 2017), also furthered understanding of the government of Puerto Rico's vision. Federal regulators at the Federal Communications Commission (FCC) also helped the team understand how current federal programs could be leveraged by Puerto Rico in its recovery efforts. In addition to federal and commonwealth partners, the team received input from Puerto Rico telecommunications providers and associations, which led to the development of additional COAs to engage the private sector to ensure commonwealth-wide provision of broadband. Finally, the team partnered with People Centered Internet and relied on the information gathered from all the already-indicated stakeholders to develop innovative COAs to address the needs of the

---

[11] Natural and Cultural Resources COAs were reviewed individually by numerous external experts rather than holistically by a single reviewer across all COAs, as done by other sectors.

[12] The *Reimagine Puerto Rico* report was the result of a series of stakeholder working groups sponsored by the Rockefeller Foundation's 100 Resilient Cities Program (Resilient Puerto Rico Advisory Commission, 2018).

Sector	Methodology
	Communications and Information Technology sector.
Community Planning and Capacity Building	The Community Planning and Capacity Building sector's COAs address capacity building in disaster preparedness, resilience building, and hazard mitigation, as well as the collection of better data for decisionmaking in these activities. The COAs also cover approaches for improving communication in recovery and the need to build local capacity in accountability and effective spending of recovery funds. The COAs were developed in partnership with FEMA's Community Planning and Capacity Building sector team and with input from the capacity-building COR3 representatives. The Community Planning and Capacity Building sector team engaged in focus groups with communities in Puerto Rico and also with communities of people who left Puerto Rico for the continental United States to learn about local needs. In addition, the team relied on academic and NGO subject-matter experts, media reports on Puerto Rico's recovery process, and consultations with public communications experts.
Economic	The Economic sector team sought to develop COAs that were broadly consistent with the government of Puerto Rico's revealed preferences, were likely feasible (because plans or proposals for specific actions existed or could be developed fairly rapidly, or they appeared in the literature), could be linked to issues raised in the DNA, and spanned the relevant policy and investment space. The Economic sector team worked jointly with the RSF Economics team to develop a list of more than 120 detailed COAs that were later aggregated to the 41 COAs included in this report. These COAs were developed by considering policy solutions and investment priorities included in planning documents published by the government of Puerto Rico, such as Plan para Puerto Rico (undated), *Build Back Better Puerto Rico* (Governor of Puerto Rico, 2017), the various fiscal plans submitted to the FOMB by the governor, the certified *New Fiscal Plan for Puerto Rico* (Government of Puerto Rico, 2018), and various presentations developed by the Department of Economic Development and Commerce and the PRIDCO. In addition, the team considered a number of economic development proposals related to specific investment projects by agencies, municipalities, and nonprofit and private-sector organizations.
Education	Early damage and needs assessment work was done in concert between the Education and the Health and Social Services sectors. As the need arose, FEMA split the two to create an independent Education sector team to help identify educational needs and review COAs. The Education sector team reviewed current needs based on available data about prekindergarten through 12th grade and postsecondary education, often working together with other sectors, such as Public Buildings (e.g., regarding school closures). In addition, the team engaged with various subject-matter experts in Puerto Rico and in other parts of the United States, including thought leaders on the topic of education reform. Insights on integrated best practices and evidence on topics—such as school development and closure policy, financing, student and teacher performance, and supportive educational services (e.g., technology or programs to bridge out-of-school time)—were used to inform COAs. Where appropriate, the team sought to develop COAs that could complement the governor's recently enacted education reform legislation (Puerto Rico Education Reform Act, 2018).
Energy	The Energy team started by examining and integrating information from extant plans, reports, and policies to harvest recommended actions and COAs that the Energy sector could follow in the rebuilding effort. These sources included the *Build Back Better Puerto Rico* plan (Governor of Puerto Rico, 2017), the Puerto Rico Electric Power Authority (PREPA) fiscal plan (2018a, 2018b), the U.S. Department of Energy One Vision Action Plan (2018a), and the *Reimagine Puerto Rico* report (Resilient Puerto Rico Advisory Commission, 2018), among others listed in Appendix A. In parallel, the team worked with federal partners, including the RSF Energy team, to document the issues identified, strategies to fix these issues, and actions proposed in support of these strategies. With this information in hand, the team collaboratively developed six sector-specific goals to ensure that all potential COAs to transform the Energy sector were captured. With a comprehensive list of COAs in support of the sector goals, the team then elicited stakeholder feedback.
Health and Social Services	The Health and Social Services sector has five subsectors (public health, health care, environmental health, mental and behavioral health, and social services), and it addressed such issues as emergency preparedness and response and recovery, as well as long-term

Sector	Methodology
	issues of resilience and systemic improvement. To address these topics, the sector team culled research and expertise in disaster response and emergency preparedness from within the team to identify best practices in key areas. In addition, the team engaged with local stakeholders and subject-matter experts in Puerto Rico, other parts of the United States, and globally to discuss the needs in Puerto Rico and possible approaches. Working with the RSF Health and Social Services team and FEMA sector leads through solution-oriented sessions, the team identified COAs and combinations of COAs that would best address needs. The team also had COAs reviewed by internal and external peer reviewers with expertise in disaster response and recovery and health systems. The team aligned COAs with priority areas identified in the *Build Back Better Puerto Rico* plan (Governor of Puerto Rico, 2017), Puerto Rico fiscal plan (Government of Puerto Rico, 2018), and related health and social services strategy documents, such as the *Chronic Disease Action Plan* developed by the Puerto Rico Department of Health (undated).
Housing	The Housing sector COAs link the approaches discussed by housing recovery stakeholders with the strategic vision and objectives as outlined by the Governor's Office, while still leaving flexibility at the implementation level. The Housing sector team developed COAs primarily based on participation in the Puerto Rico Housing Recovery Taskforce and discussions with major housing stakeholders and subject-matter experts from federal and commonwealth government agencies, nonprofit organizations, NGOs, and professional associations, including the Puerto Rico Department of Housing (PRDOH), the Puerto Rico Housing Finance Authority, the Puerto Rico Public Housing Administration, the Puerto Rico Planning Board, the Puerto Rico Mortgage Bankers Association, the Puerto Rico Homebuilders Association, HUD, and the FEMA Housing sector. Other sources were discussions with subject-matter experts from Enterprise Community Partners and other housing-focused nonprofits; Dewberry Engineers, which helped scope and cost mitigation options; and insurance experts. The team also reviewed the CDBG-DR Action Plan (Government of Puerto Rico, 2018b) and associated public forums, the 100 Resilient Cities working group and the resulting *Reimagine Puerto Rico* report (Resilient Puerto Rico Advisory Commission, 2018), resilient housing construction workshops led by Enterprise Community Partners, and the HUD (2018) document on mission-scoping assessment and recovery support strategies.
Municipalities	The Municipalities sector identified potential COAs that would address key needs related to governance, service delivery, and fiscal health at the municipal level based on major themes that emerged from 12 roundtables held with mayors; a survey conducted with all 78 municipalities; and interactions with subject-matter experts, including professors from the University of Puerto Rico's Schools of Medical Sciences, Planning, Public Administration, and Law. In addition, the Municipalities sector team consulted with and received feedback from the government of Puerto Rico's Office of the Advisor for Municipal Affairs and COR3, as well as from FEMA's Community Planning and Capacity Building and Municipalities sector teams.
Natural and Cultural Resources	The Natural and Cultural Resources sector team developed COAs using a logic model that presents the damages and needs identified (which include physical, human, and natural capital), the goals and objectives for addressing these damages and needs, and associated COAs (both strategies and actions) to attain these goals and objectives. The COAs were developed in close partnership with subject-matters experts from federal and commonwealth agencies, NGOs, academia, and private-sector organizations through several asset-focused working groups. The team prioritized areas for their ecological and economic value. These COAs incorporate local capacity development and were informed by existing plans and previous studies. The COAs seek recovery through repairs and greater integration with the education system and the economy, and, where appropriate, include actions to enhance resiliency, protect recovery investments, and build local capacity and human capital.

Sector	Methodology
Public Buildings	COAs for the Public Buildings sector address two general types of needs: (1) issues stemming directly from damage caused by Hurricanes Irma and Maria in 2017 and (2) preexisting issues that impede the efficient functioning of operations in public buildings. The Public Buildings sector team developed COAs based on needs and challenges associated with public buildings that were identified through the evaluation of hurricane damage, reviews of existing plans and initiatives, and conversations with FEMA and agencies that own public buildings in Puerto Rico. In most cases, the sector team developed COAs targeted at addressing the underlying cause of these needs and challenges.
Transportation	The Transportation sector team developed COAs based on background reading and discussions about the transportation network, conditions, and performance before and after the hurricanes, with a stronger focus on roads and ports (which move the vast majority of people and goods) than on public transit or air transportation. Specific sources included the *2040 Islandwide Long-Range Transportation Plan* (Puerto Rico Department of Transportation and Public Works, 2013), the *Build Back Better Puerto Rico* plan (Governor of Puerto Rico, 2017), and the Puerto Rico Highway and Transportation Authority fiscal plan (2018). The sector team also talked with a number of commonwealth and federal officials and experts from the Puerto Rico Department of Transportation and Public Works, the Puerto Rico Highway and Transportation Authority, the Port of Ponce, the U.S. Department of Transportation's Office of Response and Recovery, the Federal Highway Administration, the Federal Transit Administration, the Maritime Administration, the U.S. Coast Guard, the U.S. Committee on the Marine Transportation System, and the U.S. Army Corps of Engineers, as well as staff from the civil engineering department at the University of Puerto Rico, Mayaguez; the American Association of State Highway and Transportation Officials; the World Bank; and several private contractors.
Water	The Water sector team developed COAs in collaboration with a broad range of public and private agencies, organizations, and individuals with a vested interest in recovery planning efforts, as well as technical knowledge, financing, and logistical capabilities that can be leveraged to facilitate recovery. As an entry point, the team reviewed existing planning documents, such as the *Build Back Better Puerto Rico* plan (Governor of Puerto Rico, 2017) and the Puerto Rico Aqueduct and Sewer Authority's (PRASA) fiscal and capital improvement plans (2018a, 2018b). The team engaged directly with PRASA on priority recovery actions. These priorities were refined through meetings with the RSF Water sector team, where representatives from multiple federal and commonwealth agencies and NGOs have worked collaboratively to develop and evaluate alternative strategies to facilitate recovery within PRASA and non-PRASA systems, as well as stormwater and flood control infrastructure and management. The team also reviewed the *Reimagine Puerto Rico* report (Resilient Puerto Rico Advisory Commission, 2018), developed by the 100 Resilient Cities working group, and they conducted interviews with subject-matter experts in federal and commonwealth agencies, NGOs, consulting firms, and academia.

Describing and Analyzing Courses of Action

Altogether, the HSOAC sector teams developed nearly 300 COAs, which were based on hundreds of ideas that sector teams—in conjunction with stakeholders—considered, vetted, and improved through an iterative engagement process. Given the diversity of stakeholder goals and agendas, and given the diversity of the COAs themselves, there was no one dimension of merit or performance with which to evaluate the COAs. Rather, the HSOAC team devised a set of complementary approaches to analyzing the COAs and their relative alignment with government of Puerto Rico goals and priorities, as well as their sensitivity to uncertainty, their cost implications, and their potential benefits. In this way, the HSOAC team enabled government of Puerto Rico stakeholders to compare and prioritize COAs, identifying those that best aligned with their goals and thus warranted implementation.

Linking Courses of Action to the Governor's Vision

The HSOAC team, in conjunction with the government of Puerto Rico, identified a set of attributes that were consistent with the governor's vision, goals, and strategic objectives for recovery. The individual sector teams then subjectively coded each COA based on their expert knowledge on the extent to which its outcome embodied each attribute, using a categorical scale: does not apply, does not embody, partially embodies, fully embodies. A COA that *fully embodies* the attribute would satisfy all of the characteristics (described below for innovation and inclusiveness), a COA that *partially embodies* the attribute would satisfy some of the characteristics (for innovation, the COA had to be useful, usable, and novel), and a COA that *does not embody* the attribute would not meet the criteria for either fully or partially embodying the attribute.

The list of attributes originally included the following:

- **Holistic:** The COA addresses the diversity of people's psychological, physical, spiritual, and social needs.
- **Forward-looking:** The COA is undertaken in a sustainable manner. The COA meets the needs of future generations, taking into account potential for change in socioeconomic, environmental, and technological conditions. The COA will enhance community safety and well-being now and in the future. If the process of repair reveals a way of enriching people's quality of life in the future, that opportunity will be taken.
- **Inclusive:** The COA supports constructive relationships between the private sector, NGOs, local and central government agencies, and the wider community.
- **Efficiently uses resources:** The COA uses resources wisely so that the recovery is timely, affordable, and delivers value for money.
- **Innovative:** The COA harnesses technological innovation throughout rebuilding solutions and ensures that recovery decisions are guided by current science and best available data, while anticipating future uncertainties.
- **Strategically risky:** While every COA involves some risk, a COA that is strategically risky involves taking a calculated risk for a potentially large gain.

Later in the COA development process, this list of six attributes was reduced to a core set of two (innovative and inclusive) that reflected the features that the government of Puerto Rico valued most in terms of recovery planning investments. The list was reduced to enable the HSOAC sector teams to more thoughtfully code the attributes based on the best available evidence. Accordingly, the HSOAC sector teams refined their scoring process to focus exclusively on innovative and inclusive attributes.

To determine which COAs embodied innovation, the project team considered the following list of COA attributes:

- **Useful:** A COA solves a specific problem or set of problems.
- **Usable:** A COA considers cultural or social barriers to implementation.
- **Novel:** A COA does not simply repeat what has been done in the past, especially if what has been done has proven to be unsuccessful.

- **Forward-looking:** A COA has a feasible path to implementation and adoption that may take time—e.g., by maturing an emerging technology before implementation.
- **Adaptive:** A COA allows for modifications or course corrections as conditions change or as better information becomes available.

If a COA was not considered at least useful and usable, it did not appear in the final list of COAs.

To determine which COAs satisfied the inclusive attribute, the HSOAC team considered who would benefit from the results. Since community participation is crucial in disaster recovery efforts, constructive relationships are needed between the private sector, NGOs, local and commonwealth government agencies, and the wider community. A COA that *fully embodies* inclusiveness would benefit the entire population of Puerto Rico. A COA that *partially embodies* inclusiveness would benefit multiple municipalities or subpopulations but not the entire population of Puerto Rico, or it would benefit populations with limited resources to prepare for, respond to, and recover from disasters. Such populations might be characterized by the following:

- economic disadvantage (unable to stockpile supplies that may be needed during crisis and disaster)
- absence of support networks (homeless people, recent migrants, and other socially isolated groups might not be able to tap into a social support network for recovery)
- political marginalization (leading to policies that structurally discriminate against groups)
- geographical isolation (areas removed from critical transportation and telecommunications infrastructures)
- age (children or older adults)
- medical conditions (pregnancy or pharmacological, oxygen, or electrical dependency)
- disabilities (cognitive or physical)
- limited literacy.

HSOAC experts who were not on a sector team separately coded the scoring of the attributes to corroborate reliability of the scores and to mitigate bias. When scores by the independent coders and the sector teams conflicted in significant ways, the scores were adjudicated by members of a cross-sector integration team, in consultation with the sector teams.

Describing Course of Action Sensitivity to Uncertainty

The HSOAC team also qualitatively evaluated the extent to which the effectiveness and cost of each COA would be sensitive to several types of uncertainty:

- **Governance:** The current institutions, laws, and policies that govern Puerto Rico may change in the future, and some changes may affect the outcomes of COAs.
- **Climate and extreme weather:** Puerto Rico is vulnerable to a number of climate-related stressors, such as rising temperatures, changing precipitation patterns, and sea-level rise, as well as extreme weather, including hurricanes and storm surge. Uncertainties in the future frequency and severity of these conditions could affect the outcomes of COAs.

- **Economic conditions:** The local economic conditions are related to outcomes of the recovery process itself. Nevertheless, Puerto Rico's ability to recover also depends on external factors affecting local economic conditions (e.g., global economic conditions).
- **Population and demographics:** Many people have left Puerto Rico for the continental United States since the 2017 hurricanes. The total population of Puerto Rico, and its makeup, may shape the need for and effectiveness of many COAs.
- **Technology:** Technological advancements in any field can create new COAs for addressing a need, or they can change the effectiveness of existing COAs.

COA sensitivity to each type of uncertainty was coded as *none, low, medium,* or *high*. A COA was coded as low if it was deemed largely insensitive to an uncertainty, medium if it was deemed somewhat sensitive, and high if it was deemed highly sensitive.

The sector teams used their judgment to estimate the extent to which uncertainty in the factors listed above could affect the successful implementation of a COA. Sector teams were able to refer to this information when assembling portfolios, and this information remains available to help decisionmakers and implementers compare COAs at the macro level. It is important to note that, for COAs selected for implementation, a more detailed investigation of risks and uncertainties should be conducted to ensure that the specific programs and initiatives associated with those COAs can effectively mitigate the risks.

Estimating Costs of Courses of Action

The sector teams estimated the costs associated with carrying out actions or investments for most COAs.[13] In general, these were rough order-of-magnitude estimates intended to support high-level planning and inform decisionmaking. Costs were estimated for the 11-year period from fiscal year (FY) 2018 through FY 2028, which was the same time horizon of the certified *New Fiscal Plan for Puerto Rico* (Government of Puerto Rico, 2018). As we will describe, decisionmakers were able to draw on analytical tools and support during the planning process to consider groups of COAs and their total cost (i.e., affordability under a given level of available resources).

Deriving Course of Action Costs

The breadth of the sector teams' research meant there was a requirement to create cost estimates for a remarkable diversity of activities—essentially everything a modern economy

---

[13] Costs for some COAs, particularly in the Energy and Economic sectors, were often difficult to estimate. For the Economic sector, some COAs represent policies or strategies for which costs cannot be simply assigned, or for which there were not enough data. For the Energy sector, many COAs require further decisions on specific approach, level, and timing of activities that will vary depending on strategic goals and constraints. For example, for some in-progress projects, the remaining cost is uncertain and could differ by many millions to up to many billions of dollars depending on these choices. Thus, a point estimate or total cost for the Energy sector is not possible and cannot be calculated by adding the sum of the costs associated with individual COAs. The differences for these sectors is discussed in greater detail within Appendix B, immediately preceding each sector's respective COAs.

does. A separate cost team offered cross-sector guidance so that the 12 sector teams followed standardized approaches in estimating the costs of the many COAs. In most cases, sector teams estimated costs in the following categories: personnel, construction, equipment and materials, O&M, incentive payments to individuals or businesses to induce specific kinds of behavior, and transfer payments to individuals or businesses to alleviate hardship. All costs were presented in 2018 dollars, and future costs were not discounted. Some COAs would incur personnel costs only, such as training programs, emergency response planning (e.g., organizing recovery teams), programs to compile information (e.g., inventories of public buildings and cultural resources), community outreach programs, and enforcement of regulations.

The teams considered both initial costs (e.g., construction costs) and future costs (e.g., O&M) over the 11-year period. Only incremental costs associated with the recovery program were included; costs that would have been incurred anyway, in the absence of the hurricanes, were excluded. For example, facility O&M costs that were being paid before the hurricanes, and that would resume as normal once the facility was repaired, were not counted. However, if O&M costs were to increase because of structural improvements and technological upgrades, the incremental cost of these payments were tabulated. To the extent that facilities were not being maintained before the hurricane, the full O&M cost was folded into the cost of the COA.

Costs were counted only where specific expenditures are required to implement a COA and only when sufficient data were available. Costs to society associated with implementing a COA, where those costs were not specifically reimbursed by a funding source (e.g., better enforcement of regulations or reorganization of economic activity in a sector) were not counted. Some COAs had no direct costs that would require recovery funding support.[14] These were generally COAs involving policy changes, such as employment and business regulations, environmental regulations, and import and export laws. If implementing such policy changes would require hiring additional staff, specifically paid for by a recovery funding source, those employment costs were counted. Finally, some COAs were not costed by the sector teams, because of a lack of data, but they could be costed in the future, if data were to become available.

Costing Approaches

The sector teams developed COA cost estimates using multiple approaches, and they chose specific approaches based on the nature of the COAs and on available sources of information. Cost estimates were based on sector-specific features and needs. For example, Transportation sector costs included estimates for total labor, construction, and equipment costs for transit projects on a per-mile basis, as would be expected within the sector. When practical, the sector teams used a cost-transfer approach, drawing on information from past recovery efforts (e.g.,

---

[14] COAs that have no associated monetary costs, such as a policy change, may still have important nonmonetary costs related to implementation. Political costs are one example.

after Hurricanes Katrina and Sandy) and prior U.S.-based projects to improve infrastructure, housing, and community resilience. For specific infrastructure projects, sector teams drew on cost studies of similar federal and state programs. Where the cost-transfer approach was not feasible, because it was not possible to identify analogous activities or investments, sector teams constructed bottom-up estimates, drawing on unit costs from publicly available sources, as well as on project cost estimates from commercial cost-estimating resources and judgment-based estimates from subject-matter experts. In some cases, sector teams relied on existing government of Puerto Rico estimates without further analysis. Using the cost-transfer approach allowed teams to consider unique size- and location-specific aspects that affect costs. For example, construction cost estimates depend on two countervailing factors: the relatively lower cost of construction in Puerto Rico and the recovery-related surge in demand for construction.[15] Based on expert guidance, the teams assumed that these factors would be of similar magnitude and generally offset one another.

The cost estimates for the COAs are uncertain and reflect judgment-based estimates of subject-matter experts, as well as input from RSF solutions-based teams and other relevant agencies. Further, given the degree of heterogeneity in the

---

Sector-Specific Cost Factors: Communications and Information Technology

Many sectors constructed COAs that required distinct cost factors or approaches. For example, for several Communications and Information Technology sector COAs, the team estimated the cost of implementing state-of-the-art, survivable, resilient telecommunications infrastructure. Specifically, the team estimated the costs of trenching and installing conduit across Puerto Rico, through which government entities or private companies could lay buried fiber optic cable. The team used a common unit cost for trenching of approximately $10 per linear foot in flat terrain and $270 per linear foot in mountainous terrain so that costs would reflect the unique topography and challenges of construction in Puerto Rico. The team also used common cost factors for conduit, handholes, and facilities to house signal regeneration equipment.[a] Similarly, for the Public Buildings sector, the team estimated a standard new construction cost of $225 per square foot for certain classes of facilities.[b]

[a] Based on unit costs in Federal Highway Administration, 2009.
[b] Based on analysis of several classes of public buildings (e.g., schools, hospitals, police stations) using RSMeans software, including adjustments for Puerto Rico–specific cost factors.

---

[15] The Craftsman Book Company's *2018 National Building Cost Manual* (Moselle, 2017) suggests using an area modification factor of –21 percent to reflect the lower cost of construction activities in Puerto Rico. This adjustment factor is based on several construction cost variables, including labor, equipment and material costs, labor productivity, climate, job conditions, and markup.

Construction industry experts estimate that offsetting factors, including the temporary surge in demand for construction equipment and materials (including transportation), would generally be of a similar order of magnitude as commonwealth-specific construction cost factors, but in the opposite direction. For example, Engineering News-Record surveyed construction industry economists and analysts after Hurricane Katrina, who estimated that regional construction costs would increase by 10 to 20 percent in the short term (6–24 months) following the storm (Grogan and Angelo, 2005). However, construction experts indicated that cost factors for Puerto Rico were less likely to reflect surge costs than the general high cost of goods in Puerto Rico, which reflect relatively higher taxes and fuel prices.

cost methodology across sectors and COAs, COA cost estimates are presented as either a range or a single point estimate. COA costs rely on the "best estimate" for cost, as identified by the sector leads, or in cases when only a range is provided, on the arithmetic mean of the low-end and high-end cost estimates.[16] Many individual COA descriptions provide additional information on costs and uncertainty about cost estimates. Policymakers should consider these estimates to be rough order-of-magnitude, rather than bid-quality, estimates.

Personnel Costs

To estimate personnel costs, sector teams used a fully burdened labor cost that includes salary, fringe benefits, and an indirect cost factor for material, energy, and purchased services associated with employment. Sector teams estimated costs in terms of the number of persons carrying out a COA and applied a common "cost per worker" to ensure that COAs were treated consistently. For an average worker in Puerto Rico, teams applied a standard annual labor cost of $62,300. This figure is based on the total compensation of employees in the government sector, approximately $38,700 (Government of Puerto Rico, Office of the Governor, Planning Board, 2016). Based on the ratio of total compensation of employees to wages and salaries, this implies a base salary of approximately $26,400. In addition, the U.S. ratio of energy, materials, and purchased services to total compensation for state and local government (the closest available analogue) is 1.52. Applying this factor to total compensation yields a fully burdened personnel cost of $58,800, measured in 2016 dollars, or $62,300 measured in 2018 dollars, for a fully burdened employee after accounting for nominal gross domestic product (GDP) growth per worker of 6 percent. This fully burdened labor cost includes other expenses, such as office space and computers.

For projects requiring unique expertise in a technical field, such as engineers or other subject-matter experts, teams applied a standard labor cost that is double the average government rate, or $124,600. For continental U.S.–based contractors, teams used a standard annual labor cost of $227,300, which reflected a base salary of approximately $98,000 adjusted by the fully burdened cost factors described in the previous paragraph and including an additional $10,000 for travel (assuming four trips of four to five days to Puerto Rico).[17] For common "personnel only" activities, teams operated from the assumption that specific investments involved a standard number of individuals for a set duration of time, expressed in full-time equivalent (FTE) workers. Teams also anticipated that the private sector would participate in task force meetings across several sectors and, based on other private-public partnerships, would do so voluntarily

---

[16] Similarly, when combining COAs into portfolios, which will be discussed in Chapter 5, we did not propagate the uncertainty implied by the low to high range generated through the cost ranges provided by each COA. Instead, we used the best estimate (if available) or the average between low and high, when a best estimate was not available.

[17] The base salary estimate for an engineer (consultant) based in the continental United States is derived from the *Occupational Outlook Handbook* (U.S. Bureau of Labor Statistics, 2018).

and would not be compensated. Table 4.2 shows examples of common labor costs used in the development of cost estimates for the recovery plan. Sector-specific labor costs vary across COAs, and these examples are intended only to be rough order-of-magnitude estimates for the required level of effort. Where feasible, more-specific labor cost estimates were used.

Table 4.2. Examples of Common Labor Costs

Category	Average Fully Burdened Labor Cost	Rationale
Government worker (administrative)	$62,300/year	Based on compensation of government workers in Puerto Rico
Engineer/scientist/subject-matter expert	$124,600/year*	Based on discussions with government budget experts in Puerto Rico, we used a labor cost equal to double the average government rate. This estimate was also supported by the U.S. Bureau of Labor Statistics *State Occupational Employment and Wage Estimates for Puerto Rico* (2017).
Contractor based in the continental United States	$227,300/year	U.S. Bureau of Labor Statistics *Occupational Outlook Handbook* (2018)
Government workshop	$31,150	Assuming 0.5 FTE government workers (administrative)
Government training program	$311,500	Assuming 5 FTE government workers (administrative) for 1 year
Research study/task force	$1,869,000	Assuming 5 FTE subject-matter experts for 3 years
Regulatory committee	$6,230,000	Assuming 10 FTE subject-matter experts for 5 years

Construction, Equipment, and Material Costs

Many COAs will incur construction, equipment, and material costs. These include repairing damaged assets to prehurricane conditions and improving them, so they are either more disaster-resilient or meet current regulations. These COAs require construction and repair of a heterogenous set of structures, facilities, and equipment, such as the following:

- housing
- schools
- hospitals and medical clinics
- electrical generation and transmission and distribution facilities
- water treatment and wastewater treatment plants
- roads, bridges, ports, and airports
- telecommunications equipment and networks
- public buildings, including administrative and public safety buildings and museums

- natural resources, such as coral reefs and estuaries.

A consistent challenge was a lack of sufficient detail about implementation. Given the heterogenous class of structures, ideal cost estimates would be based on expert planning, facility class by facility class, in FEMA sectors and RSF teams, as well as the relevant Puerto Rico agencies. Many facilities have unique size- or location-related features that affect costs. Again, ideally, a complete physical description of an activity would have been available, including the number of people employed for planning or administrative activities and the number, square footage, and bill of materials for rebuilding, repair, and hazard-mitigation activities. The availability of such in-depth expert planning estimates varied by sector. In their absence, sector teams relied on average planning factors from publicly available or commercial cost-estimating resources and judgment-based estimates from knowledgeable sources. All cost estimates were ultimately presented to FEMA and RSFs, as well as to relevant U.S. and Puerto Rico agencies for comment and input.

Cost Analysis and Course of Action Benefits

Cost information directly supported COA analysis and decisionmaking, and the COA-specific cost estimates were well suited to higher-level analysis and cross-COA comparisons. Decisionmakers and stakeholders were able to assess COA-specific costs, rank COAs by cost, and break down costs by upfront and recurring annual costs.

That said, cost is only one dimension along which to analyze COAs, and it is often best used in conjunction with complementary outcomes measures, such as how COAs align with government of Puerto Rico goals and objectives, their sensitivity to uncertainty, and their economic impact. Cost information can help stakeholders assess the resource requirements associated with COAs, but cost information alone is not necessarily informative for priority setting, since two COAs of equal cost may meet different needs or provide different sets of benefits.

In a perfect world, all COAs would have comprehensive estimates of benefits—monetized or nonmonetized—that, when combined with cost information, would facilitate cost-benefit or cost-effectiveness analysis. That was generally not the case here. Given the project constraints and the complex nature of many investments, COAs do not have comprehensive benefit estimates. Instead, the sector teams worked under the practical, but strong, assumption that COAs identified through the iterative, expert- and stakeholder-driven process would have positive net benefits. Thus, each COA, if implemented efficiently, could potentially provide benefits greater than its cost. Supporting this assumption is the fact that some initial COAs were reviewed by stakeholders and dropped from the list of consideration when they did not meet this qualitative cost-benefit review.

Caveats for Comparing Courses of Action

COAs are nuanced and complex, and although they can be compared, such comparisons should be done carefully. COAs cover a broad set of sectors, each with distinct opportunities, challenges, and constraints. Some COAs function synergistically, while others may depend on the prior implementation of other COAs (precursors). For all these reasons, COA comparisons should take into account the full details of the COAs and not just the attributes by which they are characterized (e.g., costs, levels of uncertainty). Finally, the sheer number of these makes comparisons and prioritization difficult. As described in the next chapter, given these challenges and to enhance effective decisionmaking, the COAs were combined into consolidated alternative portfolios designed to work toward the government of Puerto Rico's recovery objectives.

5. Facilitating the Government of Puerto Rico's Development of the Recovery Plan

The extent of the hurricane damage, combined with the preexisting economic challenges, meant that the recovery actions we identified covered every aspect of a modern economy. The hundreds of COAs represent complex recovery actions that need to be understood in context with how they redress these challenges, with insights into how they connect with the key interests of inclusiveness and innovation, what their contributions will be toward meeting the 17 strategic objectives that the governor identified, and their impact on the total cost of the plan. This was a complex decisionmaking challenge. To help the government of Puerto Rico select a cohesive and effective set of COAs for its recovery plan, the HSOAC team established a decision support engagement approach supported by a unique DST developed by HSOAC for this purpose.

The DST was designed to enable the government of Puerto Rico to efficiently and effectively compare different sets of COAs designed to meet specific objectives of the Puerto Rico recovery effort. Presenting the large and varied amount of information about hundreds of possible COAs in this consolidated, consistent, and visual way allowed the government of Puerto Rico to more effectively inform and guide the approach to developing Puerto Rico's recovery plan. HSOAC did this by drafting and then vetting with the government of Puerto Rico consolidated groups of COAs, referred to as *portfolios*, that represented different alternative strategic approaches for each of the 17 strategic objectives and by populating the DST with this information.

The purpose of the DST was not to provide any single "optimal" solution but rather to support the government of Puerto Rico in engaging with a significant amount of information. This chapter describes the DST and the decision support engagements used in the development of the recovery plan.

Decision Support Tool

The DST was developed to do three things: (1) aid stakeholders in reviewing COAs, (2) support the development of portfolios by HSOAC and partners, and (3) facilitate the exploration and selection of portfolios.[18] The DST was necessary to support decisionmaking in light of the large volume of information associated with each of the COAs, the overlap or interdependencies of some COAs, and the diversity of purposes and approaches of different COAs. Further, the DST helped to track approximate total costs of the selected COAs.

---

[18] The DST front-end analytic capabilities were built in Tableau.

The DST had three main parts. The first part of the DST, organized around the 12 sectors, offered users options for reviewing information about the COAs. Figure 5.1 shows one page with the COAs from the Water sector.

Figure 5.1. Decision Support Tool Page Listing Courses of Action from the Water Sector

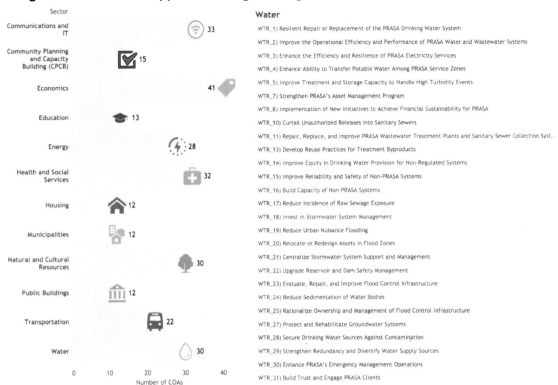

The second part of the DST summarized information about the COAs, including their relevance to government of Puerto Rico's 17 strategic objectives, so that HSOAC team members and partners could develop thoughtful portfolios of COAs that reflect different ways to approach recovery efforts in Puerto Rico.

The third part of the DST enabled government of Puerto Rico representatives to review and select portfolios to build a possible recovery plan. The DST also summed the estimated costs of COAs to produce an estimated total cost of the plan, ensuring that the cost of each COA was counted only once. Beyond costs, themes, goals, and implementation levels, portfolios also differed in terms of the attributes among the component COAs (e.g., some portfolios focused more on innovation, and others were less sensitive to future uncertainties). The DST allowed decisionmakers insight into the different characteristics of each portfolio to aid in the selection process.

Portfolios of Courses of Action to Achieve Recovery Plan Objectives

Portfolios are groups of COAs designed to meet the specific strategic objectives for the Puerto Rico recovery plan. Following a body of practical experience and academic literature, the goal of integrative efforts of portfolio-building is to ensure that scientific information effectively connects to the needs of decisionmakers—in this case, as the government of Puerto Rico decisionmakers begin to answer recovery questions (Spradlin and Kutoloski, 1999; Archer and Ghasemzadeh, 1996). Because of the short time frame available for this study, the HSOAC team was not able to develop and implement a standardized approach to creating portfolios; the team relied instead on the best expert judgment of HSOAC team members, as described below. Figure 5.2 shows how portfolios (represented by the green arrow) combine COAs (green box on the right) to meet strategic objectives (the strategic initiatives and the capital investments; see the boxes on the left). The portfolios, composed of different groupings of COAs, offer the government of Puerto Rico different ways for progressing toward the strategic objectives, which are shaped by the government of Puerto Rico's vision and goals.

Portfolios prioritize different goals depending on the selected COAs, and multiple portfolios can target the same strategic objective. For example, two portfolios may be developed for the same strategic objective, but one may prioritize the lowest cost while the other prioritizes the most resilient pathway. All the portfolios developed under a given strategic objective, therefore, represent a set of alternatives or options that the government of Puerto Rico could include in the recovery plan. Although some portfolios may include multiple COAs from only one sector, most portfolios include COAs from multiple sectors, reflecting the cross-sector integration necessary to achieve the strategic objectives.

Figure 5.2. General Depiction of How Courses of Action Are Bundled into Portfolios That Address Strategic Objectives

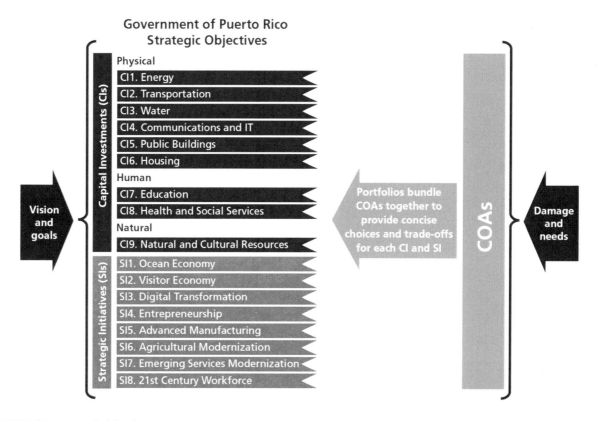

NOTE: SI = strategic initiative.

Portfolio Generation Process

The HSOAC team led the process of drafting initial portfolios of COAs for each of the 17 strategic objectives. This process was also informed by one or more meetings with government of Puerto Rico representatives or FEMA partners in which COAs and the draft portfolios were discussed. These meetings sought to thoroughly review the draft portfolios, identify missing COAs, remove unnecessary COAs, and, where relevant, revise the portfolio approaches. The overarching goal was to ensure that the portfolios represented reasonable alternatives from the perspective of cognizant Puerto Rico officials. Many engagements resulted in productive exchanges to this end, while others consisted of a brief overview and the portfolios were not necessarily revised. This occurred when engagements were limited in time or when key government of Puerto Rico and FEMA partners were not able to be involved because of the short time available for this task.

For the capital investment portfolios, the HSOAC team corresponding to the sector most closely related to the topic developed the portfolios (e.g., the Housing sector team developed the housing portfolios). These teams drafted portfolios that factored in results of the DNA (Fischbach et al., 2020) and accounted for precursors and interdependencies across sectors. Given the many ways in which COAs could be combined together to create portfolios, the teams drew on their expertise and engagement with external stakeholders. Therefore, the process for developing these portfolios generally followed a more bottom-up approach, in which the sector teams' primary goal was to create cohesive portfolios that accurately reflected the recovery needs for their sectors. Portfolios often include both COAs from the primary sector (e.g., Housing-sector COAs for the housing objective) and COAs from other sectors necessary to meet the vision of that portfolio (so a housing portfolio may include COAs from the Water, Energy, and Transportation sectors). Specific COAs may be critical for, and appear in, multiple portfolios, but the DST ensured that the costs of these COAs were counted only once as the total cost estimate of the plan was developed.

For the strategic initiative portfolios, the project team used a cross-sector approach, in which one or more HSOAC team members with knowledge of the issues pertaining to the initiative developed the portfolios. In most cases, representatives from the sectors most closely related to the objective built the portfolio (e.g., the Communications and Information Technology and Community Planning and Capacity Building sectors developed the Emergency Services Modernization and Integration portfolio). Since the strategic initiatives that make up the strategic objectives do not align with the 12 sectors, these cross-sector HSOAC teams created portfolios by starting from the strategic objectives and working downward, combining COAs through a top-down approach.

Once the teams reviewed the COAs that were potentially relevant to achieving each objective, they combined the relevant COAs in a new portfolio and suggested new COAs where they perceived gaps. The portfolios for the capital investment and strategic initiative objectives were used in the engagement process with the government of Puerto Rico and provided as possible building blocks for the recovery plan.

Portfolios Developed

Tables 5.1 and 5.2 provide the combined set of portfolios that the project team created for the decision support engagement with the GAR,[19] ordered from lowest to highest cost by sector. Portfolios under each strategic objective were developed to meet different goals, approaches, or levels of implementation. For example, the Transportation capital investment includes a potential portfolio named a Focus on Resilience, which includes COAs that effectively support resilience (e.g., projects to harden or relocate vulnerable transportation infrastructure assets), in addition to two other alternative portfolios for that objective. Alternatively, the Visitor Economy strategic objective includes three alternative portfolios focused on three levels of implementation (essentials, big push, highly comprehensive). The description of the portfolio that was ultimately chosen for the recovery plan is italicized. There are also portfolios that focus on precursor COAs

---

[19] The GAR was appointed to the COR3 by the governor in February 2018 to be the state leader in the Hurricane Maria recovery effort, reporting to the governor directly.

that are needed to support other COAs and portfolios; these are primarily focused on the Economic sector.

Table 5.1. Capital Investment Portfolios

Strategic Objective	Key Sectors	Portfolio Alternatives Presented
Physical Capital		
Energy	ENR	**Lower Cost**: Focus on repair of hurricane damages (lower-cost option).
		Power to Choose Energy: Focus on enabling local distributed energy generation and "customer choice" community-level infrastructure (e.g., microgrids).
		Energy to Support Critical Infrastructure: Focus investments on public service facilities (e.g., hospitals), critical (physical) infrastructure (i.e., transportation, telecommunications, and water), and interdependent systems.
		Energy to Power (Industrial) Economic Development: Focus on supporting industry, prioritizing resilient transmission-power quality, and reducing price volatility. Assumes on-site generation or microgrids at industrial sites.
		Moonshot Energy: Build the "smart grid of the future": high renewables, highly resilient (e.g., to disasters), and highly connected and automated.
Transportation	TXN, CIT, ENR, HOU, NCR, WTR	**Focus on Future Maintenance:** Assume Puerto Rico gets a one-time cash infusion and comes up with best possible transportation infrastructure without increasing maintenance and repair requirements.
		Focus on Resilience: Focus on investments in existing infrastructure rather than new capacity. The primary benefit is in upgrading vulnerable assets to be more storm resilient.
		Support Industry Tourism and Good Movement: Use specific projects to improve movement of goods and commuting. The goal is to spur domestic production and consumption.
Water	WTR, CIT, CPCB, ENR, HSS, HOU, MUN, NCR	**Basic:** Assume a resource-constrained environment that limits recovery efforts to addressing critical failures caused by hurricane damage.
		Transitional: Assume a resource-rich environment enabled by large federal investments and recovery of Puerto Rico's economy.
		Transformational: Assume sufficient resources are available to address hurricane damage and the chronic challenges in water and wastewater services.
Communications and Information Technology	CIT	**Resilient Communications:** Implement a state-of-the art survivable resilient telecommunications infrastructure for continuity of government functions and for the provision of public safety to the residents of Puerto Rico. This infrastructure will include a robust data center to store and manage data on critical public infrastructure and with connections to redundant core (cloud) centers.
		Driver of Economic Growth: Partner with the private sector to implement a state-of-the art survivable resilient telecommunications infrastructure to provide commercial telecommunications services, including telephone and data services, to the residents of Puerto Rico.

Strategic Objective	Key Sectors	Portfolio Alternatives Presented
		This infrastructure will support affordable commonwealth-wide access to broadband to spur economic growth.
		Smart and Resilient Island IT and Communications: Make use of information technology to further the economic and social vitality of the commonwealth; foster government and private-sector innovation; increase economic opportunity; and help improve quality of life for the residents of Puerto Rico.
Public Buildings	PBD, HOU, MUN, NCR	**Efficiency but No Resilience:** Repair and improve the efficiency of buildings, but do not pursue other actions, such as improved resilience.
		Resilience but No Efficiency: Repair and maintain buildings resistant to future disasters, but do not pursue other actions, such as efficiency improvements.
		Repair and Right-Size: Repair and maintain a right-sized amount of buildings to code.
		Reform: Repair and maintain a right-sized amount of buildings to code and build out modernized services under the appropriate ownership structures.
Housing	HOU, CIT, CPCB, ENR, HSS, MUN, NCR, PBD, TXN, WTR	**Basic Recovery:** Focus on fixing what is damaged and moving people out of harm's way. This approach only partially positions Puerto Rico housing to better withstand future storms.
		Housing Resilience: Fix what is damaged and attempt to right some structural challenges to housing that limit the ability of the sector to be more resilient at a larger scale.
		Broad-Scale Housing Resilience: Make a larger investment in mitigating homes that did not experience substantial damage but are not built to current codes.
Human Capital		
Education	EDU, PBD, CIT	**Strengthen Education Systems to Support the Governor's Education Reforms:** Repair, update, and upgrade schools and strengthen systems to support Governor's education reform.
		Direct Support for Students and Teachers: Repair, update, and upgrade damaged schools and provide direct support for students and teachers.
		Student Support + Strengthen System + Technology: Repair, update, and update schools; strengthen systems to support the governor's education reform; provide direct support for teachers and students; and improve technology in education.
Health and Social Services	HSS, CIT, CPCB, EDU, ENR, HOU, MUN, NCR, PBD, TXN, WTR	**Increase Flexibility in Service Access for Vulnerable Populations:** Create greater flexibility to ensure that food health and other social supports are provided or continued for populations disproportionately affected by disaster.
		Strengthen and Expand Workforce for Health and Social Services: Combine COAs related to licensure incentives and nontraditional health providers with emergency preparedness COAs to strengthen and expand access to health and social services.
		Improve Consistent Data-Quality Monitoring and Data Infrastructure: Link key elements of data systems and integration of data systems that track factors that promote or detract from health and well-being.

Strategic Objective	Key Sectors	Portfolio Alternatives Presented
		Build Systems and Supports for Health Promoting Communities: Create multisector conditions that support health and well-being through community attributes design changes and other aspects of environmental and community conditions.
		Building Robust and Healthy Communities: Combine key COAs from other four Health and Social Services portfolios to address overarching themes but also aims at being streamlined.
Natural Capital		
Natural and Cultural Resources	NCR	**Cheap Insurance Policy:** Provide minimal recovery of assets and the infrastructure protection and water-quality functions they provide.
		Subject-Matter Expert Benchmark: Essential recovery of assets (excluding parks) to provide infrastructure protection, water quality, recreation, and economic opportunities but not improve resiliency. Prioritize sites that provide the maximum value for investment.
		Comprehensive Insurance Plan: Provide comprehensive recovery of assets and the infrastructure protection water quality recreational and economy-related functions they provide and prioritizes sites that provide the maximum value for investment.
Precursors		
Precursors	ECN, MUN, CPCB	**Precursors:** Focus on Economic sector prerequisite COAs for the recovery plan.
		Precursors Additional: Focus on additional precursor COAs from non–Economic sectors.

NOTES: The description of the portfolio that was ultimately chosen for the recovery plan is italicized. CIT = Communications and Information Technology sector; CPCB = Community Planning and Capacity Building sector; ECN = Economic sector; EDU = Education sector; ENR = Energy sector; HOU = Housing sector; HSS = Health and Social Services sector; MUN = Municipalities sector; NCR = Natural and Cultural Resources sector; PBD = Public Buildings sector; TXN = Transportation sector; WTR = Water sector.

Table 5.2. Strategic Initiative Portfolios

Strategic Objective	Key Sectors	Portfolio Alternatives Presented
Ocean Economy (BLUEtide)	ECN, EDU, HSS, MUN, NCR, PBD	**Ocean Essential:** Includes elements essential to rebuilding the ocean economy and beginning to implement the BLUEtide initiative. **Ocean Big Push:** Expands on the Ocean Essential portfolio and includes additional COAs intended to develop a more integrated approach to growing the ocean economy in a resilient, sustainable direction. ***Ocean Comprehensive:*** *Builds on the Ocean Big Push portfolio and represents a robust implementation of the BLUEtide initiative. Combines multiple elements designed to work together to encourage and sustain economic growth and innovation in fishing tourism trade and other economic areas surrounding Puerto Rico's ocean economy.*
Visitor Economy	CPCB, ECN, EDU, HSS, MUN, NCR, PBD	**Visitor Economy Essential:** Represents foundational elements necessary to redevelop the tourism industry in Puerto Rico. Focuses on recovering assets and capacity lost during the hurricanes. **Visitor Economy Big Push:** Builds on the Visitor Economy Essential portfolio and includes additional COAs that help the tourism sector grow and become more resilient in coastal areas while beginning to reach the interior of Puerto Rico. Expands tourism opportunities in parallel with recovery of key assets and infrastructure, as well as develops a budding market for business tourists. ***Visitor Economy Comprehensive:*** *Builds on the Visitor Economy Big Push portfolio to include a robust set of COAs aimed at generating a resilient, sustainable visitor economy that spans all of Puerto Rico. Begins to set the conditions for evolving tourism opportunities into lasting business opportunities, including attracting visitors to stay and live in Puerto Rico.*
Digital Transformation	CPCB, ECN, EDU, HSS, MUN, NCR	**Digital Reform and Government Modernization:** Modernizes government processes and improves citizen services to increase efficiency and improve coordination for recovery and preparedness. **Seeding the Innovation Economy:** Modernizes government and expands access to the internet, new technologies, and digital skills to citizens to create conditions for an innovation ecosystem. ***Technology-Empowered Governance:*** *Leverages advances in data collection storage and analysis to improve decisionmaking regarding public assets and policy issues and position the government as the technology leader and innovator in Puerto Rico.*
Entrepreneurship	CPCB, ECN, EDU, NCR, PBD	**Broad Focus:** Promotes business and economic growth with broad policy changes and investments in workforce energy and the other necessary infrastructure. **Attract Top Talent:** Encourages migration to Puerto Rico, particularly among populations likely to create job growth in the commonwealth. **Natural and Cultural Tourism:** Capitalizes on the natural resources of Puerto Rico to grow business in such industries as agriculture fisheries and tourism and ensure that the natural political and human capital resources are available to do so. **Small-Business Focus:** Grows small businesses by reducing barriers and red tape, developing workforce skills, and investing directly into small businesses. ***Encourage Entrepreneurship:*** *Merges separate portfolios (Attract Top Talent, Small-Business Focus, and Facilitate Organic Growth), which were selected by the government of Puerto Rico as portfolios of interest.*

Strategic Objective	Key Sectors	Portfolio Alternatives Presented
		Facilitate Organic Growth: Uses educational and vocational programs to develop the Puerto Rican workforce. Uses business incubators to support new business development.
Advanced Manufacturing	CPCB, ECN, EDU, HSS, MUN, NCR, PBD	**Advanced Manufacturing Essential:** Implements COAs fundamental to the development of advanced manufacturing in Puerto Rico. *Advanced Manufacturing Big Push: Builds on the Advanced Manufacturing Essential portfolio and adds COAs designed to develop, attract, and retain a workforce and attract foreign investment in advanced manufacturing in Puerto Rico.* **Advanced Manufacturing Comprehensive:** Builds on the Advanced Manufacturing Big Push portfolio, including adding a set of COAs intended to attract and retain labor, attract foreign investment, and position Puerto Rico as the center of advanced manufacturing in the Caribbean.
Agricultural Modernization and Processing	CPCB, ECN, HSS, NCR, PBD	**Smaller Agriculture Support Levels:** Partly implements the Build Back Better strategy at roughly 50 percent, along with minimal additions necessary for the agricultural sector. Designated cheapest option among agricultural portfolios. *Agricultural Sustainable Growth: Addresses (1) a lack of critical mass to achieve greater productive capacity for both domestic consumption and export, (2) outdated farming practices that fail to attract a younger workforce to sustain operations long term, and (3) insufficient access to capital as an industry that stifles entrepreneurialism and growth.* **Big Agriculture Investment:** Invests heavily in agriculture and all related COAs to make a big push (designed for a world without constraints). **Sustainable Agricultural Growth:** Focuses on sustainable production methods with low resource use, ensures local farmers collaborate to maximize yield and revenues from exports and local farmers' markets, and promotes Puerto Rican products in niche high-end grocers and restaurants. **Build Back Better Plus:** Implements the Build Back Better strategy at 100 percent, along with some strategic additions for the agricultural sector.
Emergency Services Modernization and Integration	CPCB, ECN, HSS, MUN, NCR, PBD	**Fundamental Activities in Support of Improving Emergency Services:** Focuses on improving Puerto Rico's capacity to respond to emergencies at commonwealth and municipal levels in key areas, such as adequate emergency response staffing preparedness improvement and emergency communications. *Improving Community Capacity and Resilience to Support Emergency Services: Recognizes that emergency services are needed to support hardest-hit communities during a disaster but are always stretched thin during a major disaster. To maximize emergency resources, it is important to mitigate impacts of disaster through resilience-building activities.*
Twenty-First Century Workforce	CPCB, ECN, EDU, ENR, HSS, MUN, NCR, PBD	**Lower-Cost Human Capital:** Gets currently unemployed adults back to the workforce but does not provide building blocks for a sustainable human capital development plan. Designated cheapest option or returning to the status quo among workforce portfolios. **Policies for a Workforce Development System:** Includes policies necessary to support a workforce development system. **Plan and Design of a Workforce Development System:** Includes assessments, analysis, and initiatives to design a strong, agile workforce development system.

Strategic Objective	Key Sectors	Portfolio Alternatives Presented
		Address Short-Term Employment: *Meets the short-term employment needs of currently unemployed workers and invests in strategies to train and "skill up" vulnerable populations and workers (e.g., youth, women, veterans) in high-need occupations, such as middle-skill jobs in the health care, construction, energy, and information technology sectors.*
		Support Long-Term Workforce Development System: Takes a strategic and systemic approach to developing a pool of talent in Puerto Rico that is employable in high-priority occupations across multiple sectors in a way that aligns and adapts with an evolving labor market.

NOTES: The description of the portfolio that was ultimately chosen for the recovery plan is italicized. These portfolios originally included COAs from the infrastructure-related sectors—Energy, Water, Transportation, Communications and Information Technology, and Housing. During the iterative engagement process, it was determined that they were better described as sets of COAs that build on the infrastructure recovery COAs. CPCB = Community Planning and Capacity Building sector; ECN = Economic sector; EDU = Education sector; ENR = Energy sector; HSS = Health and Social Services sector; MUN = Municipalities sector; NCR = Natural and Cultural Resources sector; PBD = Public Buildings sector.

Decision Support Engagements

HSOAC led decision support engagements using the DST with the government of Puerto Rico (COR3 and cabinet-level representatives), FEMA representatives, and other key stakeholders. The engagements were organized around a particular strategic objective to enable portfolio exploration, and decisionmakers were given the opportunity to consider the merits of the various portfolios. Then, the HSOAC team conducted deeper follow-up engagements with stakeholders at the commonwealth and federal levels to assess, discuss, and augment the various portfolio options for most of the strategic objectives, as time allowed. The goal of these engagements was to enable key stakeholders to refine the portfolios (or develop their own) to match their vision. The DST supported this process by providing visualizations that summarized the COAs and their attributes.

Reviewing Portfolios

When analyzing portfolios, decisionmakers had the opportunity to understand and compare the different investments and ways to achieve recovery goals. The HSOAC team explained that each portfolio was an alternative way to achieve a specific objective (capital or strategic) that was both feasible and relevant. To explore the portfolio options, the DST was designed to allow decisionmakers to read the brief description of each portfolio and then review the contents and mix of sectors and COAs represented to gain an awareness of the differences between the alternative portfolios. Decisionmakers engaged in portfolio review used this approach to varying degrees. Figure 5.3 shows an example of DST visualization for the capital investment portfolios for the Water sector that demonstrates an approach a decisionmaker could take to assess a portfolio alternative. The figure shows the name and description of the objective and portfolios;

41

the cost of implementing the COAs in the portfolio; the distribution of COAs across sectors included in the portfolios, weighted by cost (pie charts); and a listing of all the COAs included in the portfolios, with the size of the icon indicating the level of implementation.

Figure 5.3. Portfolio Overview (Courses of Action and Costs) Visualization in the Decision Support Tool, Showing the Portfolios for the Water Strategic Objective

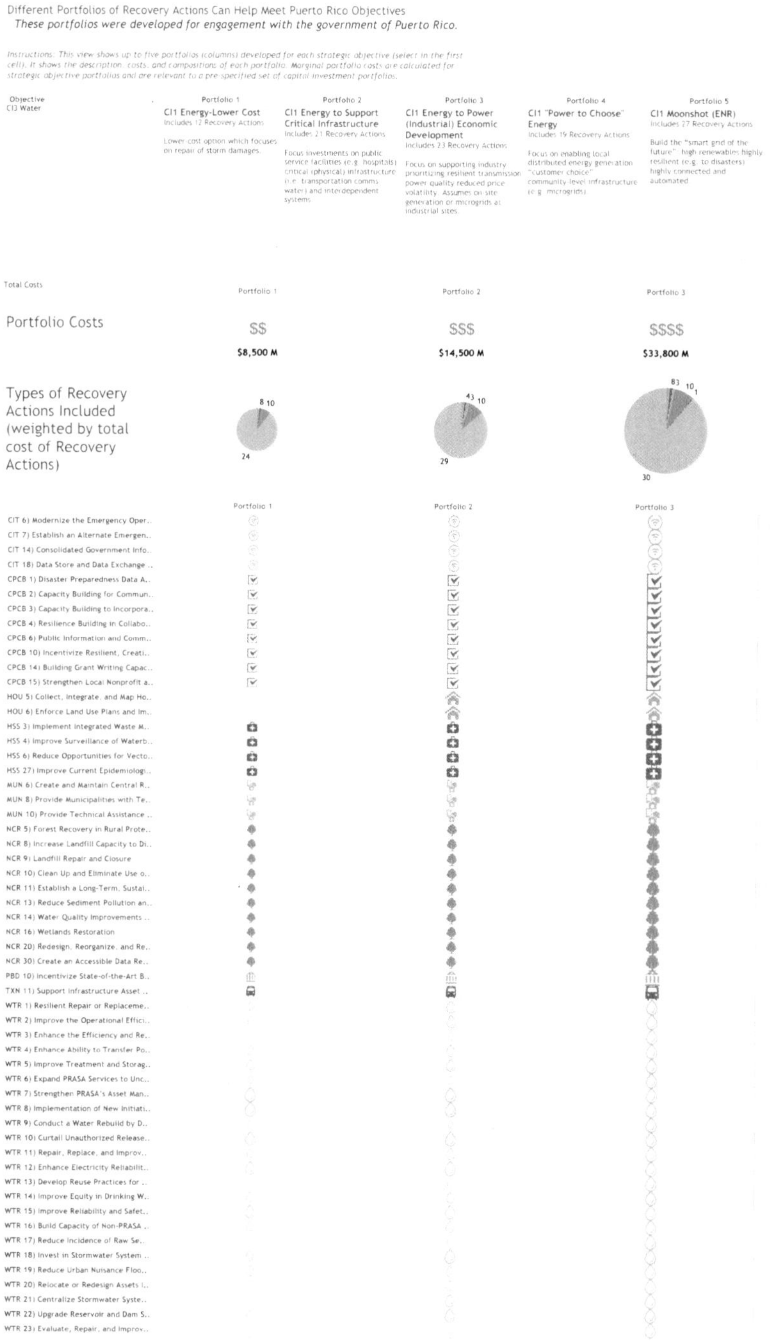

Different Portfolios of Recovery Actions Can Help Meet Puerto Rico Objectives
These portfolios were developed for engagement with the government of Puerto Rico.

Instructions: This view shows up to five portfolios (columns) developed for each strategic objective (select in the first cell). It shows the description, costs, and composition of each portfolio. Marginal portfolio costs are calculated for strategic objective portfolios and are relevant to a pre-specified set of capital investment portfolios.

Objective (3) Water	Portfolio 1	Portfolio 2	Portfolio 3	Portfolio 4	Portfolio 5
	CI1 Energy–Lower Cost	CI1 Energy to Support Critical Infrastructure	CI1 Energy to Power (Industrial) Economic Development	CI1 "Power to Choose" Energy	CI1 Moonshot (ENR)
	Includes 12 Recovery Actions	Includes 21 Recovery Actions	Includes 23 Recovery Actions	Includes 15 Recovery Actions	Includes 27 Recovery Actions
	Lower cost option which focuses on repair of storm damages.	Focus investments on public service facilities (e.g. hospitals) critical (physical) infrastructure (i.e. transportation comms water) and interdependent systems.	Focus on supporting industry prioritizing resilient transmission power quality reduced price volatility. Assumes on site generation or microgrids at industrial sites.	Focus on enabling local distributed energy generation "customer choice" community-level infrastructure (e.g. microgrids)	Build the "smart grid of the future": high renewable; highly resilient (e.g. to disasters) highly connected and automated

Total Costs	Portfolio 1	Portfolio 2	Portfolio 3
Portfolio Costs	$$	$$$	$$$$
	$8,500 M	$14,500 M	$33,800 M

NOTES: This figure is truncated; the DST includes additional rows for COAs. The size of an icon indicates the level of implementation, and each sector has its own icon. SI = strategic initiative.

42

Using the DST, decisionmakers could consider portfolios based on the aggregate attributes, uncertainties, and costs of the underlying COAs. For instance, a decisionmaker might have been most interested in portfolios that scored highly on innovation. The decisionmaker could examine the different portfolios for a strategic objective and focus only on those that scored the highest on COAs that embodied the principle of innovation. Also, because current and future conditions that are beyond the control of decisionmakers will influence Puerto Rico's recovery, the merits of different portfolios may be sensitive to a variety of uncertainties about the future. For example, a decisionmaker could analyze a particular portfolio of ten COAs, with five that were highly sensitive to climate and extreme weather and economic conditions and two that were somewhat sensitive to economic conditions. The decisionmaker could use this information to consider adjusting the choice of COAs to reduce sensitivities to specific uncertainties. During the decision support engagements, described below, these options for assessing portfolios were presented to decisionmakers, but HSOAC did not have visibility into which of these features were ultimately used to make portfolio decisions.

In most cases, decisionmakers from the government of Puerto Rico worked with HSOAC team experts to review draft portfolios in the workshop setting. Generally, the government of Puerto Rico and federal decisionmakers designated by the GAR or FEMA to a specific strategic objective would begin by reviewing the COAs within their fields of expertise and then reviewing all the other COAs sector by sector to see which COAs were best suited for incorporation into the selected portfolio. Most teams used the DST alongside printed versions of the COAs to facilitate this process. In some cases, decisionmakers made edits in real time by suggesting COAs to add, remove, or replace. Some also requested new portfolios aimed at achieving a specific vision. In other cases, decisionmakers took the list of COAs from the meeting and provided feedback later about edits and new portfolios.

Selecting Portfolios for the Recovery Plan

Once government of Puerto Rico representatives and other federal stakeholders had the opportunity to refine portfolio choices, the GAR from the COR3 selected the final set of portfolios for the plan. There were multiple choices for each of the 17 investment priorities, with a total of 61 different portfolio options to build a complete recovery plan guided by the governor's vision.[20] When selecting the portfolios, the GAR identified a portfolio for each strategic objective, which, when combined, would create a recovery plan that would accomplish the vision for Puerto Rico's recovery. The costs of the portfolios were considered, but no explicit budget constraint was adhered to. To ensure costs are not double counted, the DST includes only

---

[20] There is also an additional set of precursor portfolios, but these are always included, so we do not include them in the count of portfolios.

43

the estimated cost of a COA once,[21] even when the COA is included in more than one selected portfolio. Once all portfolios were selected, the total cost was reviewed and deemed acceptable by the GAR.

In the first decision support engagement facilitated by HSOAC, the GAR selected the portfolios for capital investments, followed by a subsequent engagement to review and select the strategic initiative portfolios. Sometimes, multiple portfolios were selected by the GAR in a given strategic initiative, with a request to combine the portfolios. In these instances, representatives from the government of Puerto Rico, with the support of the project team and federal partners, reviewed the individual COAs within the preferred portfolios to develop a single portfolio for the strategic objective that more closely aligned with the government of Puerto Rico's vision.

The portfolios were selected by the GAR on the basis of the portfolio name and description, theme, included COAs, and estimated cost. Individual COAs within the portfolios were not independently added or removed, but portfolio-development teams were provided an opportunity following the decision engagements to refine the mix of COAs while remaining aware of the preferred vision by the GAR and COR3. The GAR and other participants were reminded of the approximate and preliminary nature of the COAs and portfolios, as well as the need for further analysis following the publication of the recovery plan (Governor of Puerto Rico, 2018a) to explore underlying assumptions, cost estimates, and likely consequences of implementation.

HSOAC's goal in these decision support engagements to facilitate portfolio selection for the plan was to expose trade-offs and help senior government of Puerto Rico officials understand how subject-matter experts view the portfolios after broad consultation with external partners at the project level, as well as to home in on the government of Puerto Rico's most-critical priorities. Even though the decisionmaking process emphasized by the GAR looked for the most-beneficial outcomes, decisions still involved evaluating trade-offs, making value-based choices, and assessing feasibility. For instance, many of the portfolios contained COAs for governance and policy actions that might have been precursors or interdependencies for other COAs to be effective. Accounting for and ensuring the feasibility of policy changes that may be necessary to implement some COAs when selecting portfolios was an essential component of the decisionmaking process. The DST was used to help the government of Puerto Rico explore trade-offs between what is included in the plan and the total cost of the plan.

Refining the Final Recovery Plan

Once the GAR selected the preferred portfolios, HSOAC helped incorporate the precursors and interdependencies among COAs. Many COAs included in the plan were costed in more

---

[21] If different levels of implementation are selected for the same COA, the DST chooses the most extensive implementation level.

detail, when possible, by the HSOAC sector teams, and HSOAC and FEMA further explored funding sources to try to identify all funding sources across the sectors (e.g., identifying needs for and sources of matching funds). In addition, the sector teams and other federal and commonwealth stakeholders scrutinized the COAs within the portfolios in more detail. During this process, the Economic sector removed economics-related COAs from the capital investment portfolios because they were intended to represent companion programs rather than capital investments. These economics-related COAs were instead incorporated as precursors to capital investment portfolios or included in portfolios that supported the strategic initiatives.

Also, the sector teams determined that the critical infrastructure COAs included in the strategic initiative portfolios should be removed. This better reflected the way in which the DST was used—first to select portfolios to recover the essential infrastructure components and second to select portfolios to achieve the strategic initiatives. The government of Puerto Rico followed the advice of HSOAC and cognizant subject-matter experts to view the strategic initiative portfolios as a set of potential visionary approaches for achieving the strategic objectives rather than a set plan of confirmed COAs. Following this decision, government of Puerto Rico representatives, external subject-matter experts, and HSOAC researchers reviewed all the portfolios within each strategic initiative for their overall alignment with the government of Puerto Rico's vision and best practices. This resulted in some significant changes in portfolios. For example, one portfolio alternative was removed that did not align with analytical evidence and the government of Puerto Rico's visions and best practices.

After the portfolios were finalized with the HSOAC sector teams, COR3 reviewed the individual COAs within the portfolios in detail to ensure that they reflected the government of Puerto Rico's vision for Puerto Rico. This process occurred as the recovery plan was being finalized. HSOAC supported COR3 in making edits, and HSOAC's sector subject-matter experts advised COR3 representatives as necessary to ensure any changes to the COAs did not change any of the intent behind them. These subject-matter experts continued to stay involved with COR3 throughout the writing of the recovery plan to provide any further analytical support to the governor's vision. The final recovery plan delivered to Congress reflected the decisions of the governor (Governor of Puerto Rico, 2018a).

Identifying Funding Sources

The HSOAC team identified potential funding sources for each of the COAs, including funding from the federal government and other sources. Note that this work did not result in a formal funding *plan*, which would require generating commitments from funders. For this effort, the HSOAC team identified three broad categories of potential funding to meet the estimated costs of the recovery plan:

- funding known to be available

- funding for which the amount available is known but the amount that Puerto Rico will receive is uncertain
- funding that will have to be sought from additional sources and for which success obtaining these funds is not guaranteed.

To the extent that the sum totals of COAs included in the recovery plan exceeded available U.S. government resources, the team also considered alternate, nongovernmental funding sources, including philanthropic sources, the private sector, and expected private insurance reimbursements. Specifically, at the strategic objective level, the team identified alternate sources of funding and associated them with the type of investments the alternative sources might be able to support.

6. Summary and the Way Forward

This report describes HSOAC's process of gathering information and conducting analysis to support Puerto Rico's strategic plan for repairing damage from the hurricanes and addressing longer-term economic recovery needs. It also provides the COAs that the project team developed in conjunction with other organizations (see Appendix B). The report was developed as part of the planning process to meet the requirement—stated in the Further Additional Supplemental Appropriations for Disaster Relief Requirements Act, 2018 (Pub. L. 115-123, 2018)—that the governor of Puerto Rico submit to Congress a report describing the commonwealth's 12- and 24-month economic and disaster recovery plans. The report was compiled in collaboration with the COR3, other offices and agencies of the Commonwealth of Puerto Rico, FEMA, other federal agencies, HSOAC, Deloitte, the University of Puerto Rico, and dozens of other experts in disaster and economic recovery. We also incorporated input from the municipalities of Puerto Rico and numerous public workshops.

This effort was carried out along two tracks. First, HSOAC developed an independent DNA to document pre- and posthurricane conditions in the wake of Hurricanes Irma and Maria. Other assessments required by statute and often along different timelines as specified by the Stafford Act and other legislation informed this assessment (Fischbach et al., 2020; Pub. L. 100-707, 1988).[22] Some of these other requirements were separate from the 180-day requirement for this plan, as specified in the Further Additional Supplemental Appropriations for Disaster Relief Requirements Act, 2018 (Pub. L. 115-123, 2018).[23]

Second, as the DNA was being written, the project team documented the vision, goals, and strategic objectives of the government of Puerto Rico. HSOAC drew on existing documents, such as the "build back better" request for federal disaster recovery assistance (Governor of Puerto Rico, 2017), the Plan para Puerto Rico (undated), and the *New Fiscal Plan for Puerto Rico* (Government of Puerto Rico, 2018). These documented analyses were complemented by interaction with the government of Puerto Rico staff to refine the vision, goals, and strategic objectives for the specific purpose of the recovery plan.

Simultaneously, HSOAC and federal partners began developing potential COAs. This effort entailed coordination with or gathering information from RSFs, FEMA sectors, COR3 staff, municipal leaders, NGOs, and other stakeholders to gather and assess ideas for Puerto Rico's economic and disaster recovery. The project team described the nearly 300 COAs using a

---

[22] Many of these other formal assessments have not been completed at the time of writing. See the DNA for details on data gaps.

[23] It is also important to note that response and initial recovery activities were ongoing while this plan was being developed.

common template. For each COA, the project team estimated the costs that would likely be incurred to carry out relevant actions or investments to the extent possible and practical within the time constraints of the project. For each COA, the project team, with support from external partners, identified potential sources of funding for implementation.

To make the range of choices more manageable for decisionmakers, HSOAC bundled these COAs into portfolios that were aligned with the strategic objectives. HSOAC worked with the government of Puerto Rico and stakeholders through a guided engagement process to refine portfolios and, in some cases, generate new COAs to fill gaps identified through those discussions. This process included facilitated activities to understand the dependencies of the portfolios on features or factors that are risky or uncertain. The decision support engagements with stakeholders allowed portfolio exploration, which ultimately helped determine which initiatives and approaches the government of Puerto Rico included in its recovery plan. The refinement of the portfolios and COAs continued throughout the recovery plan's building process with the government of Puerto Rico, leading up to the delivery of the plan to Congress on August 8, 2018 (Governor of Puerto Rico, 2018a). This iterative process ensured that the government of Puerto Rico was able to present the plan that best reflected its vision for the future of Puerto Rico.

HSOAC drafted multiple versions of the recovery plan itself. After HSOAC's final delivery of the draft recovery plan to the government of Puerto Rico in late July, the governor's team directed the inclusion of additional material that connected with other communications by the governor, in an effort to best align with the vision for Puerto Rico he put forth. HSOAC incorporated the requested government of Puerto Rico changes to ensure that the plan was fully aligned with his vision (with the exception being some wording changes that would indicate action by a federal government agency when that agency had not previously agreed to that action). Because of the timing of these requested changes (shortly before the final plan was due), there was insufficient time to conduct the necessary analyses to connect them to the recovery actions described in the rest of the plan, and thus these are not reflected in the COAs listed in the plan, and they are not included in the cost estimate for recovery. This material is included in Chapter 2 of the plan, "A Vision for Puerto Rico," which lays out the governor's vision for the future of Puerto Rico.

The plan was signed by the governor of Puerto Rico and submitted to Congress on August 8, 2018, as required in the congressional language. On August 28, 2018, the FOMB announced that it certified the plan as submitted (FOMB, 2018).

Appendix A. Sources Used in Course of Action Development, by Sector

Source	CIT	CPCB	ECN	EDU	ENR	HSS	HOU	MUN	NCR	PBD	TXN	WTR
American Association of State Highway and Transportation officials											X	
Area Maritime Security Committee											X	
BLUEtide initiative			X									
Build Back Better Puerto Rico (Governor of Puerto Rico, 2017)	X		X	X	X	X	X		X	X	X	X
Central Office of Recovery, Reconstruction, and Resiliency (COR3)	X	X	X	X	X	X	X	X	X	X	X	X
Climate Change Adaptation Plan (U.S. Environmental Protection Agency, 2014)									X			
Community Development Block Grant– Disaster Recovery public forums							X					
Community focus groups		X				X						
Community focus groups[a]		X										
Congressional Task Force on Economic Growth in Puerto Rico												X
Consejo Multisectoral						X						
Cultural Resources Advisory Committee									X			
Dewberry Engineers							X					

49

Source	CIT	CPCB	ECN	EDU	ENR	HSS	HOU	MUN	NCR	PBD	TXN	WTR
DHS Puerto Rico Communications/ IT Solutions Based Team (FEMA Communications/ IT Solutions-Based Team, 2018)	X											
Domestic and international communications and information technology pilot programs	X											
Dynamic Itinerary for Infrastructure Projects Public Policy Document (MP Engineers of Puerto Rico, 2008)												
Elper-Wood International									X			
Enterprise Community Partners							X					
Environmental Quality Board									X			
External subject-matter expertise	X	X		X	X	X	X	X	X	X		X
Federal Communications Commission (FCC)	X											
Federal Highway Administration											X	
Federal Transit Administration											X	
FEMA Communications and Information Technology sector RSF	X											
FEMA Community Planning and Capacity Building sector		X						X				
FEMA Economic sector			X									
FEMA Education sector				X								
FEMA Energy sector					X							

Source	CIT	CPCB	ECN	EDU	ENR	HSS	HOU	MUN	NCR	PBD	TXN	WTR
FEMA fuel planning documentation					X							
FEMA Health and Social Services sector RSF				X		X						
FEMA Housing Sector Data Integration Team							X					
FEMA Municipalities sector RSF								X				
FEMA Natural and Cultural Resources sector									X			
FEMA Water sector												X
Fiscal plans for Puerto Rico			X	X	X	X					X	
Foundation for Puerto Rico		X										
GeoAdaptive									X			
Government of Puerto Rico Water sector priorities												X
Hazard mitigation plan review		X										
Heritage Emergency National Task Force									X			
Housing Damage Assessment and Recovery Strategies Report (HUD, 2018)							X					
HSOAC subject-matter experts	X	X	X	X	X	X	X	X	X	X	X	X
HUD							X					
HUD and PRDOH Jointly Organized Housing Recovery Taskforce							X					
Hurricane Maria Communications Task Force's *DR-4339-PR Consolidated Communications Restoration Plan* (2017)	X											

Source	CIT	CPCB	ECN	EDU	ENR	HSS	HOU	MUN	NCR	PBD	TXN	WTR
Institute for Energy Economics and Financial Analysis, *Toward Electric System Sustainability in Puerto Rico* (Torres and Kunkel, 2018)					X							
Institute of Puerto Rican Culture									X			
Inter-American University				X					X			
Long-range transportation plan (Puerto Rico Department of Transportation and Public Works, 2013)											X	
Maritime Administration											X	
Media reports[a]		X										
Municipal assessments							X	X				
Museum of Art of Puerto Rico									X			
NASA									X			
National Oceanic and Atmospheric Administration (NOAA)									X			X
Natural and Cultural Resources Working Group									X			
New Fiscal Plan for Puerto Rico (Government of Puerto Rico, 2018)			X	X	X	X	X				X	
New York Federal Reserve			X									
Outmigrant focus groups[a]		X										
Para la Naturaleza interviews and reports									X			
People Centered Internet												

Source	CIT	CPCB	ECN	EDU	ENR	HSS	HOU	MUN	NCR	PBD	TXN	WTR
Plan and special regulation for the special planning area of Carso (by the Puerto Rico Planning Board)												X
Plan para Puerto Rico (undated)			X		X							
PRASA												X
PRASA's capital improvement plan for fiscal years 2016–2020 (PRASA, 2018b)												X
PRASA's master plan update (PRASA, 2014)												X
PRASA's *Revised Fiscal Plan to Incorporate Modifications to the Certified Fiscal Plan as a Result of the Impact of Hurricanes Irma and Maria* (PRASA, 2018a)												X
PRASA's *Water and Wastewater Master Plan* (PRASA, 2011)												X
PREPA fiscal plans (PREPA, 2017, 2018b)			X		X							
PREPA Integrated Resource Plan (PREPA, undated)					X							
PREPA requests for proposals					X							
PREPA revised fiscal plan (2018a)					X							
PREPA Transformation Advisory Council					X							
PRIDCO			X							X		
Private contractors[a]					X				X		X	X
Public communications expert consultation		X										
Puerto Rican Museum of Contemporary Art									X			

Source	CIT	CPCB	ECN	EDU	ENR	HSS	HOU	MUN	NCR	PBD	TXN	WTR
Puerto Rico Broadband Task Force	X											
Puerto Rico Climate Change Council's *State of the Climate 2010–2013* (2013)									X			
Puerto Rico Department of Department of Economic Development and Commerce			X									
Puerto Rico Department of Health						X						
Puerto Rico Department of Housing							X					
Puerto Rico Department of Natural and Environment Resources									X			X
Puerto Rico Department of Natural Resources and Environment, *Forest Action Plan* (2016a)									X			
Puerto Rico Department of Natural Resources and Environment's water plan (2016b)												X
Puerto Rico Department of Natural Resources and Environment's wildlife and conservation plan (2015)									X			
Puerto Rico Department of Public Health												X
Puerto Rico Department of Public Safety	X											
Puerto Rico Department of Sports and Recreation									X			

Source	CIT	CPCB	ECN	EDU	ENR	HSS	HOU	MUN	NCR	PBD	TXN	WTR
Puerto Rico Department of Transportation and Public Works											X	
Puerto Rico Disaster Recovery Action Plan for the Use of CDBG-DR Funds in Response to 2017 Hurricanes Irma and Maria (Governor of Puerto Rico, 2018b)			X				X					
Puerto Rico Energy Working Group, *Build Back Better: Reimagining and Strengthening the Power Grid of Puerto Rico* (2017)					X							
Puerto Rico Highway and Transportation Authority (2018)											X	
Puerto Rico Homebuilders Association							X					
Puerto Rico Housing Finance Authority							X					
Puerto Rico Mortgage Bankers Association							X					
Puerto Rico Office of the Chief Information Officer	X											
Puerto Rico Office of the Chief Innovation Officer	X											
Puerto Rico Planning Board							X			X		
Puerto Rico Public Buildings Authority										X		
Puerto Rico Public Housing Administration							X					
Puerto Rico Science Technology and Research Trust												X

Source	CIT	CPCB	ECN	EDU	ENR	HSS	HOU	MUN	NCR	PBD	TXN	WTR
Puerto Rico State Historic Preservation Office									X			
Puerto Rico State Office of Energy					X							
Puerto Rico Tele-communications Regulatory Board	X											
Puerto Rico Tourism Company									X			
Puerto Rico Water Supply Supervision Program Revised Enforcement and Compliance Strategic Plan for Non-PRASA Public Water Systems (Puerto Rico Department of Health, Assistant Secretariat of Environmental Health, 2015)												X
Puerto Rico—A Way Forward (Krueger, Teja, and Wolfe, 2015)			X									
Puerto Rico's integrated solid waste management strategy									X			
Reforma Puerto Rico									X			
Reimagine Puerto Rico report (Resilient Puerto Rico Advisory Commission, 2018)					X	X	X		X			X
Repair or Rebuild: Options for Electric Power in Puerto Rico (Campbell, Clark, and Austin, 2017)					X							
Roundtables on tourism[a]			X									
Roundtables with municipal mayors[a]								X				
RSF Capacity Building team		X										

Source	CIT	CPCB	ECN	EDU	ENR	HSS	HOU	MUN	NCR	PBD	TXN	WTR
RSF Community Planning team		X										
RSF Infrastructure Systems					X							
RSF Natural and Cultural Resources									X			
Solar and Energy Storage Association (SESA) of Puerto Rico's Puerto Rico Energy Summit, San Juan, June 25–26, 2018					X							
Tele-communications providers	X											
Transportation Research Board											X	
U.S. Army Corps of Engineers											X	
U.S. Coast Guard											X	
U.S. Committee on the Maritime Transportation System											X	
U.S. Department of Agriculture					X				X			
U.S. Department of Energy					X							
U.S. Department of Energy, *Energy Resilience Solutions for the Puerto Rico Grid* (2018b)					X							
U.S. Department of Energy, National Labs					X							
U.S. Department of Homeland Security's infrastructure protection sector characterization studies (see Regional Resiliency Assessment Program, 2014)					X							

Source	CIT	CPCB	ECN	EDU	ENR	HSS	HOU	MUN	NCR	PBD	TXN	WTR
U.S. Department of Homeland Security's *Public Safety Communications Summary Report* (Interoperable Communications Technical Assistance Program, 2018b)	X											
U.S. Department of Homeland Security's *Public Safety Communications Summary Report* (Interoperable Communications Technical Assistance Program, 2018a)	X											
U.S. Department of Transportation											X	
U.S. Department of Transportation, Office of Response and Recovery											X	
U.S. Environmental Protection Agency					X	X			X			X
U.S. Forest Service									X			
U.S. National Park Service									X			
University of Puerto Rico					X	X		X	X		X	
World Bank			X								X	

NOTES: CIT = Communications and Information Technology sector; CPCB = Community Planning and Capacity Building sector; ECN = Economic sector; EDU = Education sector; ENR = Energy sector; HOU = Housing sector; HSS = Health and Social Services sector; MUN = Municipalities sector; NCR = Natural and Cultural Resources sector; PBD = Public Buildings sector; TXN = Transportation sector; WTR = Water sector.
[a] The sector-specific volumes have more-detailed information on the specific sources.

Appendix B. Course of Action Descriptions

Appendix B is available for download at www.rand.org/t/RR2597. The COAs are listed by sector and are all included in the recovery plan.

References

Archer, Norman P., and F. Ghasemzadeh, *Project Portfolio Selection Techniques: A Review and a Suggested Integrated Approach*, Hamilton, Ohio: Michael G. DeGroote School of Business, Innovation Research Centre, 1996. As of February 4, 2019:
http://hdl.handle.net/11375/5415

Barnes, M. D., C. L. Hanson, L. M. Novilla, A. T. Meacham, E. McIntyre, and B. C. Erickson, "Analysis of Media Agenda Setting During and After Hurricane Katrina: Implications for Emergency Preparedness, Disaster Response, and Disaster Policy," *American Journal of Public Health*, Vol. 98, No. 4, 2008, pp. 604–610.

Campbell, Richard J., Corrie E. Clark, and D. Andrew Austin, *Repair or Rebuild: Options for Electric Power in Puerto Rico*, Washington, D.C.: Congressional Research Service, R45023, November 16, 2017. As of October 30, 2018:
https://fas.org/sgp/crs/row/R45023.pdf

Dewar, James A., *Assumption-Based Planning: A Tool for Reducing Avoidable Surprises*, Cambridge, UK: Cambridge University Press, 2002.

DHS—*See* U.S. Department of Homeland Security.

Federal Emergency Management Agency, *FEMA Operational Planning Manual*, P-1017, Washington, D.C., June 2014.

———, *FEMA Operational Planning Keystone*, Washington, D.C., P-1035, August 2015.

———, "Puerto Rico Disaster Declaration as of 11/01/2017," Washington, D.C., FEMA-4339-DR, 2017. As of April 24, 2017:
https://gis.fema.gov/maps/dec_4339.pdf

Federal Highway Administration, *Rural Interstate Corridor Communications Study: Report to States*, Washington, D.C., February 2009.

FEMA—*See* Federal Emergency Management Agency.

FEMA Communications/IT Solutions-Based Team, *DHS Puerto Rico Communications/IT Solutions Based Team*, Washington, D.C.: Federal Emergency Management Agency, June 30, 2018, Not available to the general public.

Financial Oversight and Management Board, "Unanimous Written Consent Certifying the Recovery Plan Submitted by the Governor of Puerto Rico to the US Congress Pursuant to the Bipartisan Budget Act of 2018," August 28, 2018. As of February 18, 2019:
https://drive.google.com/file/d/1SlKkgO5WTZi5gqN6H6PV9wKypZbPDoxc/view

Fischbach, Jordan R., Linnea Warren May, Katie Whipkey, Shoshana R. Shelton, Christine Anne Vaughan, Devin Tierney, Kristin J. Leuschner, Lisa S. Meredith, Hilary J. Peterson, and HSOAC Puerto Rico Recovery Team, *After Hurricane Maria: Predisaster Conditions, Hurricane Damage, and Recovery Needs in Puerto Rico*, Santa Monica, Calif.: RAND Corporation, RR-2595-DHS, 2020. As of September 21, 2020:
https://www.rand.org/pubs/research_reports/RR2595.html

Government of Puerto Rico, *New Fiscal Plan for Puerto Rico*, San Juan, 2018. As of April 25, 2018:
http://www.aafaf.pr.gov/assets/newfiscalplanforpr-01-24-18.pdf

Government of Puerto Rico, Office of the Governor, Planning Board, *Statistical Appendix to the Economic Report for the Governor and Legislative Assembly*, San Juan, 2016.

Governor of Puerto Rico, *Build Back Better Puerto Rico: Request for Federal Assistance for Disaster Recovery*, San Juan: Government of Puerto Rico, November 2017. As of April 24, 2018:
https://www.governor.ny.gov/sites/governor.ny.gov/files/atoms/files/Build_Back_Better_PR.pdf

———, *Transformation and Innovation in the Wake of Devastation: An Economic and Disaster Recovery Plan for Puerto Rico*, San Juan: Government of Puerto Rico, August 2018a. As of February 4, 2019:
http://www.p3.pr.gov/assets/pr-transformation-innovation-plan-congressional-submission-080818.pdf

———, *Puerto Rico Disaster Recovery Action Plan for the Use of CDBG-DR Funds in Response to 2017 Hurricanes Irma and Maria*, San Juan: Government of Puerto Rico, 2018b. As of February 4, 2019:
http://www.cdbg-dr.pr.gov/wp-content/uploads/2018/07/HUD-Approved-Action-Plan_EN.pdf

Grogan, Tim, and William J. Angelo, "Katrina Keeps Inflation Roaring," *Engineering News-Record: Third Quarterly Cost Report*, September 2005, pp. 66–68.

Groves, David G., Jordan R. Fischbach, Debra Knopman, David R. Johnson, and Katheryn Giglio, *Strengthening Coastal Planning: How Coastal Regions Could Benefit from Louisiana's Planning and Analysis Framework*, Santa Monica, Calif.: RAND Corporation, RR-437-RC, 2014. As of February 4, 2019:
https://www.rand.org/pubs/research_reports/RR437.html

Houston, J. Brian, Joshua Hawthorne, Milfred Perreault, Eun Hae Park, Marlo Goldstein Hode, Michael Halliwell, Sarah E. Turner McGowen, Rachel Davis, Shivani Vaid, Jonathan Mcelderry, and Stanford A. Griffith, "Social Media and Disasters: A Functional Framework for Social Media Use in Disaster Planning, Response, and Research," *Disasters*, Vol. 39, No. 1, 2015, pp. 1–22.

HUD—*See* U.S. Department of Housing and Urban Development.

Hurricane Maria Communications Task Force, *DR-4339-PR Consolidated Communications Restoration Plan*, October 2017.

Interoperable Communications Technical Assistance Program, *Public Safety Communications Summary Report*, Washington, D.C.: U.S. Department of Homeland Security, 2018a.

———, *Puerto Rico Public Safety Communications Summary and Recommendations Report*, Washington, D.C.: U.S. Department of Homeland Security, 2018b.

Joint Chiefs of Staff, *Joint Planning*, Washington, D.C., Joint Publication 5-0, June 2017.

Krueger, Anne O., Ranjit Teja, and Andrew Wolfe, *Puerto Rico—A Way Forward*, San Juan: Government Bank for Puerto Rico, 2015. As of May 10, 2019:
http://www.bgfpr.com/documents/FinalUpdatedReport7-13-15.pdf

Lempert, Robert J., Steven W. Popper, David G. Groves, Nidhi Kalra, Jordan R. Fischbach, Steven C. Bankes, Benjamin P. Bryant, Myles T. Collins, Klaus Keller, Andrew Hackbarth, Lloyd Dixon, Tom LaTourrette, Robert T. Reville, Jim W. Hall, Christophe Mijere, and David J. McInerney, *Making Good Decisions Without Predictions: Robust Decision Making for Planning Under Deep Uncertainty*, Santa Monica, Calif.: RAND Corporation, RB-9701, 2013. As of January 28, 2019:
https://www.rand.org/pubs/research_briefs/RB9701.html

Littlefield, Robert, and Andrea Quenette, "Crisis Leadership and Hurricane Katrina: The Portrayal of Authority by the Media in Natural Disasters," *Journal of Applied Communication Research*, Vol. 35, No. 1, 2007, pp. 26–47.

Milken Institute School of Public Health, George Washington University, *Ascertainment of the Estimated Excess Mortality from Hurricane María in Puerto Rico*, Washington, D.C., 2018.

Moselle, Ben, ed., *2018 National Building Cost Manual*, Carlsbad, Calif.: Craftsman Book Company, 2017.

Moser, Susanne, "The Contextual Importance of Uncertainty in Climate-Sensitive Decision Making: Toward an Integrative Decision-Centered Screening Tool," in Thomas Dietz and David Bidwell, eds., *Climate Change in the Great Lakes Region: Navigating an Uncertain Future*, East Lansing: Michigan State University Press, 2012, pp. 179–212.

MP Engineers of Puerto Rico, P.S.C., *Dynamic Itinerary for Infrastructure Projects Public Policy Document*, San Juan, May 2008. As of April 8, 2019:
http://www.ads.pr.gov/files/2013/05/Dynamic_Itinerary.pdf

National Research Council, *Informing Decisions in a Changing Climate. Panel on Strategies and Methods for Climate-Related Decision Support*, Washington, D.C.: The National Academies Press, 2009.

Plan para Puerto Rico, "Modelo de transformación socioeconómico," undated.

Public Law 100-707, Robert T. Stafford Disaster Relief and Emergency Assistance Act, November 23, 1988. As of February 12, 2019:
https://www.govinfo.gov/content/pkg/STATUTE-102/pdf/STATUTE-102-Pg4689.pdf

Public Law 113-2, An Act Making Supplemental Appropriations for the Fiscal Year Ending September 30, 2013, to Improve and Streamline Disaster Assistance for Hurricane Sandy, and for Other Purposes, January 23, 2013. As of February 12, 2019:
https://www.govinfo.gov/app/details/PLAW-113publ2

Public Law 114-187, Puerto Rico Oversight, Management, and Economic Stability Act, June 30, 2016. As of February 14, 2019:
https://www.govinfo.gov/app/details/PLAW-114publ187

Public Law 115-123, H.R. 1892—Bipartisan Budget Act of 2018, February 9, 2018. As of February 11, 2019:
https://www.congress.gov/bill/115th-congress/house-bill/1892/text

Puerto Rico Aqueduct and Sewer Authority, *Water and Wastewater Infrastructure Master Plan*, San Juan, 2011.

———, *Water and Wastewater Infrastructure Master Plan*, San Juan, 2014.

———, *Revised Fiscal Plan to Incorporate Modifications to the Certified Fiscal Plan as a Result of the Impact of Hurricanes Irma and Maria*, San Juan, April 2018a. As of April 9, 2019:
http://www.aafaf.pr.gov/assets/20180405-prasa-revised-fiscal-plan-working-draft-as-of-april-5%2C-2018-v1-final.pdf

———, "Capital Improvement Plan (CIP)," webpage, last updated July 12, 2018b. As of December 5, 2018:
http://www.acueductospr.com/investors/Investors_cip.html

Puerto Rico Climate Change Council, *Puerto Rico's State of the Climate 2010–2013: Assessing Puerto Rico's Social-Ecological Vulnerabilities in a Changing Climate*, San Juan, 2013. As of November 10, 2018:
http://pr-ccc.org/download/PR%20State%20of%20the%20Climate-FINAL_ENE2015.pdf

Puerto Rico Department of Health, *Chronic Disease Action Plan 2014–2020*, San Juan, undated. As of April 8, 2019:
https://www.iccp-portal.org/sites/default/files/plans/Puerto%20Rico%20Chronic%20Disease%20Action%20Plan%20English.pdf

Puerto Rico Department of Health, Assistant Secretariat of Environmental Health, *Puerto Rico Water Supply Supervision Program Revised Enforcement and Compliance Strategic Plan for Non-PRASA Public Water Systems*, San Juan, 2015.

Puerto Rico Department of Natural Resources and Environment, *State Wildlife Action Plan: Ten Year Review*, San Juan, September 2015. As of April 8, 2019:
http://drna.pr.gov/historico/PRSWAP2015.pdf?set_language=es-pr&cl=es-pr

———, *Forest Action Plan*, San Juan, 2016a. As of April 8, 2019:
http://drna.pr.gov/wp-content/uploads/2016/12/SAP-2016-FINAL-9-15-2016-rev-ETI.compressed.pdf

———, *Plan Integral de Recursos de Agua de Puerto Rico*, San Juan, 2016b. As of April 8, 2019:
http://drna.pr.gov/wp-content/uploads/formidable/PIRA-2016.pdf

Puerto Rico Department of Transportation and Public Works, *2040 Islandwide Long Range Transportation Plan*, San Juan, December 2013.

Puerto Rico Education Reform Act, No. 85-2018, March 29, 2018. As of April 8, 2019:
http://www.oslpr.org/download/en/2018/A-085-2018.pdf

Puerto Rico Electric Power Authority, "Plan Integrado de Recursos (Integrated Resource Plan)," webpage, undated. As of June 12, 2019:
https://aeepr.com/es-pr/QuienesSomos/Paginas/ley57/Plan-Integrado-de-Recursos.aspx

———, *2017 Fiscal Plan*, San Juan, April 28, 2017. As of April 8, 2019:
http://www.aafaf.pr.gov/assets/fiscal-plan---pr-electric-power-authority.pdf

———, *Amended Fiscal Plan—Draft*, San Juan, April 5, 2018a. As of April 8, 2019:
http://www.aafaf.pr.gov/assets/prepa-fiscal-plan-(v_april)-4.5.18.pdf

———, *2018 Fiscal Plan*, San Juan, August 1, 2018b. As of December 2, 2018:
https://aeepr.com/es-pr/Documents/Exhibit-1-FiscalPlan_(PREPA)-20180801.pdf

Puerto Rico Energy Working Group, *Build Back Better: Reimagining and Strengthening the Power Grid of Puerto Rico*, New York, December 2017. As of May 29, 2019:
https://www.governor.ny.gov/sites/governor.ny.gov/files/atoms/files/PRERWG_Report_PR_Grid_Resiliency_Report.pdf

Puerto Rico Highway and Transportation Authority, *PRHTA Fiscal Plan—Draft*, April 5, 2018. As of April 9, 2019:
http://www.aafaf.pr.gov/assets/prhta-fiscal-plan---2018-04-05-vpublic.pdf

PRASA—*See* Puerto Rico Aqueduct and Sewer Authority.

PREPA—*See* Puerto Rico Electric Power Authority.

Regional Resiliency Assessment Program, *Puerto Rico Resiliency Assessment Report*, Washington, D.C.: Office of Infrastructure Protection, U.S. Department of Homeland Security, 2014.

Resilient Puerto Rico Advisory Commission, *Reimagine Puerto Rico*, San Juan, 2018. As of May 5, 2018:
http://www.resilientpuertorico.org/en/

Spradlin, C. Thomas, and David M. Kutoloski, "Action-Oriented Portfolio Management," *Research-Technology Management*, Vol. 42, No. 2, April 1999, pp. 26–32.

Tierney, K., C. Bevc, and E. Kuligowski, "Metaphors Matter: Disaster Myths, Media Frames, and Their Consequences in Hurricane Katrina," *The ANNALS of the American Academy of Political and Social Science*, Vol. 604, No. 1, 2006, pp. 57–81.

Torres, Tomás J., and Cathy Kunkel, *Toward Electric System Sustainability in Puerto Rico*, Cleveland, Ohio: Institute for Energy Economics and Financial Analysis, March 2018.

U.S. Bureau of Labor Statistics, *State Occupational Employment and Wage Estimates for Puerto Rico*, May 2017. As of April 8, 2019:
https://www.bls.gov/oes/2017/may/oes_pr.htm

———, *Occupational Outlook Handbook*, Washington, D.C., last updated April 13, 2018.

U.S. Department of Energy, *One Vision Action Plan for Power Restoration for Puerto Rico*, Washington, D.C., last updated January 2018a.

———, *Energy Resilience Solutions for the Puerto Rico Grid*, Washington, D.C., last updated June 2018b. As of April 8, 2019:
https://www.energy.gov/sites/prod/files/2018/06/f53/DOE%20Report_Energy%20Resilience%20Solutions%20for%20the%20PR%20Grid%20Final%20June%202018.pdf

U.S. Department of Homeland Security, *National Disaster Recovery Framework*, 2nd ed., Washington, D.C., 2016. As of April 25, 2018:
https://www.fema.gov/media-library-data/1466014998123-4bec8550930f774269e0c5968b120ba2/National_Disaster_Recovery_Framework2nd.pdf

———, *2017 Hurricane Season FEMA After-Action Report*, Washington, D.C., July 12, 2018. As of April 8, 2019:
https://www.fema.gov/media-library-data/1531743865541-
d16794d43d3082544435e1471da07880/2017FEMAHurricaneAAR.pdf

U.S. Department of Housing and Urban Development, *Housing Damage Assessment and Recovery Strategies Report Puerto Rico*, Washington, D.C., June 29, 2018. As of March 23, 2019:
http://spp-pr.org/wp-content/uploads/downloads/2018/07/HUD-Housing-Damage-
Assessment-Recovery-Strategies-6-29-18.pdf

U.S. Environmental Protection Agency, *Climate Change Adaptation Plan*, June 2014. As of April 8, 2019:
https://www.epa.gov/sites/production/files/2015-08/documents/adaptationplans2014_508.pdf